ᴬLIVING SACRIFICE

Unsung Heroes of Adventist Missions

A LIVING SACRIFICE

Unsung Heroes of Adventist Missions

D. J. B. Trim

Pacific Press®
Publishing Association
Nampa, Idaho | www.pacificpress.com

Cover design by Gerald Lee Monks
Cover design resources from iStockphoto.com
Inside design by Gerald Lee Monks

The author assumes full responsibility for the accuracy of all facts and quotations as cited in
this book.

Additional copies of this book are available for purchase by calling toll-free 1-800-765-6955
or by visiting http://www.adventistbookcenter.com.

Library of Congress Cataloging-in-Publication Data

Names: Trim, D. J. B. (David J. B.), author.
Title: A living sacrifice : unsung heroes of Adventist missions / D. J. B. Trim.
Description: Nampa, Idaho : Pacific Press Publishing Association, [2019]
Identifiers: LCCN 2019006147 | ISBN 9780816365340 (pbk. : alk. paper)
Subjects: LCSH: General Conference of Seventh-day Adventists—Missions. |
   General Conference of Seventh-day Adventists—History. |
   Missionaries—Biography. | Self-sacrifice.
Classification: LCC BV2495 .T75 2019 | DDC 266/.6732—dc23 LC record available at
   https://lccn.loc.gov/2019006147

May 2019

Dedicated

to my mother, Mary Trim

Therefore, I urge you, brothers and sisters, in view of God's mercy, to offer your bodies as a living sacrifice, holy and pleasing to God—this is your true and proper worship. Do not conform to the pattern of this world, but be transformed by the renewing of your mind. Then you will be able to test and approve what God's will is—his good, pleasing and perfect will.

—Romans 12:1, 2, NIV

But where, oh where are the men who have love enough for the truth and precious souls to give themselves with unselfish devotion to the work? Men are wanted who are willing to leave their farms, their business, and their families, if need be, to become missionaries . . . to go into foreign lands . . . in hope of sowing the seeds of truth. . . .
     . . . The warning of a soon-coming Judgment [is] yet to be given to all nations, tongues, and peoples, yet where are the men who are willing to make any and every sacrifice to get the truth before the world?

—Ellen G. White, *Historical Sketches of the Foreign Missions of the Seventh-day Adventists,* 164

Table of Contents

Acknowledgments

I am very grateful to Jim Nix, who is a friend as well as a colleague. He was responsible for organizing the 2018 Leadership Education and Development (LEAD) Conference, which preceded the Annual Council of the General Conference executive committee in Battle Creek, Michigan. He was also responsible for inviting me to give the keynote address. That invitation offered an opportunity to complete and crystallize research on missionary sacrifice that I had developed during the previous seven years. It also gave me the privilege of learning more about—and then sharing with today's church leaders—the many stories of extraordinary (and largely forgotten) sacrifice that laid the foundations for the worldwide Seventh-day Adventist Church of the twenty-first century.

After the lecture, I appreciated Jim's gracious comments and those of a number of other colleagues, including Audrey Andersson, Bill Knott, Gary Krause, Michel Lee, Rick McEdward, Jerry and Janet Page, Magdiel Pérez Schulz, Ella Simmons, Clinton and Gina Wahlen, and Nancy and Ted Wilson. Their affirmation encouraged me to develop the hour-long address at Battle Creek into a book. Dale Galusha also supported this project; he has my profound gratitude, as do Miguel Valdivia, Scott Cady, and the rest of the team at Pacific Press®, for making this book a reality.

All historical research involves collaborative effort. Several individuals have assisted me, but Ashlee Chism, in particular, has been invaluable: She assisted with researching the archival records and church periodicals that helped me in writing the initial drafts for the Battle Creek keynote address. She found most of the photographs in this book—many of which come from old and little-explored photographic collections and will be unfamiliar to readers. And she read and commented on a completed draft of the book. I offer her my wholehearted thanks. For the photographs of missionaries' grave sites, I am grateful to Stefan Höschele and Gideon Reyneke. I am indebted to Benjamin Baker and Guilherme Brasil de Souza for their assistance in checking church publications. For granting permission to use photographs from their collections, I gratefully acknowledge the Ellen G. White Estate, the Center for Adventist Research at Andrews University, and Loma Linda University's Department of Archives and Special Collections.

I also want to thank Wendy Trim, who read and commented on parts of the drafts of the Battle Creek address and on sections of the book manuscript. She helped me, as she does so often, to say what I was trying to say but more clearly.

Finally, I end by noting my gratitude and lifelong debt to my mother, Mary Trim. She served as a missionary in foreign countries; read me stories of missionaries when I was a child, thus kindling an admiration for David Livingstone and Eric B. Hare, among others; published poetry and stories (under the pen name Marye Trim) and literary and historical scholarship; with my late father, taught me to be a committed Seventh-day Adventist Christian; and instilled in me a love of history. This book in many ways reflects her influence. I dedicate it to her with filial love.

David J. B. Trim
May 2019

PART 1
Remembering

CHAPTER 1

About Eva

On November 3, 1920, Eva May Clements died in Rangoon, the capital of Burma (now Yangon, Myanmar). We know little of Eva's life; we do not even have a photograph. She was born in 1897, near Bundaberg on the eastern coast of Queensland, Australia. We know nothing more about her until September 1914, when, at the age of sixteen, Eva took a position in the headquarters of the Australasian Union Conference, near Sydney. She worked there for more than five years in a stenographic and secretarial role; in January 1920, she was called to serve as a stenographer (administrative assistant) for the president of the Southern Asia Division in Lucknow, India. Today, the church would not call an international service employee to work in a clerical capacity. But in 1920, there were merely a thousand members across the whole of India, and there may not have been a believer in India who had stenographic expertise in English and was familiar with the language of denominational administration—and so the division called for a missionary stenographer.[1]

SS *Mantua*. Photo credit: Alan C. Green, State Library of Victoria (Australia).

The fact that the call went to Eva suggests something about her character and that she was good at her job. So does the fact that when people spoke of Eva, they described her as "devoted to her work" and to the Adventist message.[2]

Eva accepted the call, and so, on March 3, 1920, she departed Sydney on the P&O Steam Navigation Company's SS *Mantua*, sailing for Bombay via Melbourne and Colombo. Having landed in Bombay (the former name of Mumbai), she traveled by train on the 880-mile journey to Lucknow, where she arrived safely on March 29. It had been only eighty-four days since the General Conference executive committee had voted to approve John E. Fulton's suggestion that Australia "supply a stenographer to India."[3] Fulton had only arrived in India the previous year but had been president of the Australasian Union Conference from 1909 to 1916 and knew Eva. It is likely that he proposed she, in particular, be sent as the stenographer. If so, it suggests that she may have been interested in mission service earlier.[4]

John E. Fulton.

Eva seems to have settled well in Lucknow. According to her obituary, "She entered heartily into her work at the Lucknow office, and much enjoyed life," and was popular among her new colleagues, thanks to a "bright disposition, [and] spirit of helpfulness." A former colleague in Sydney recalled that, in her letters, she had "no complaints to make concerning the climate or environment [culture] in India." In one such letter, Eva wrote, "I want to tell you that I am glad I came to India."[5]

She had, however, been there for five months when, around August 31, she left with Fulton's wife, on a trip to Burma (then part of the Southern Asia Division), intending to meet John Fulton in Rangoon, as he was then in southern India. Susie and Eva traveled first by rail from Lucknow to Calcutta (today's Kolkata), then by ship to the port town of Moulmein in southeast Burma, and finally, by boat up the great Salween River to the remote town of Kamamaung. They stayed there for two to three weeks with the Fultons' daughter Agnes and her husband, Eric B. Hare, who later became legendary for his mission stories. Lucknow was a huge city—a center of civilization for centuries and celebrated by the famous author Rudyard Kipling. But in Kamamaung, they were eighty miles from the nearest Europeans. Eva must have thought that she was really getting into the mission field! She and Mrs. Fulton enjoyed their time there, but Eva suffered from a fever. Yet it seemed to pass; in October, they moved to Rangoon, where they met Pastor Fulton, who had a series of meetings, culminating in a ten-day general meeting of the Burma Union Mission at the end of the month.[6]

Although absent from the office, Fulton was still conducting presidential business. In early October, Eva Clements was kept busy with his correspondence; later in the month, as Mrs. Fulton later recalled, Eva spent much time "writing programmes for meetings and copying budgets." Eva kept up this work, Susie Fulton wrote, "almost to the day she went to the Hospital."

Eric B. Hare.

For unfortunately, Eva had to be admitted to the Rangoon General Hospital for appendicitis. On the penultimate morning of the union session, Sabbath, October 30, her appendix was removed, apparently without complications. Rangoon General Hospital was a modern institution, and she ought to have recovered. But the fever she contracted in Kamamaung in September had greatly weakened Eva, and on visiting her before the operation, the Fultons noted that, though "quite cheerful," she was anxious "that her illness might terminate fatally."[7]

Sadly, her concern was justified. On the night of the October 31, she slipped into a coma. She never regained consciousness. In the early morning of November 3, 1920, she passed away. Without the strain and sickness arising from her missionary service, Eva would almost certainly have successfully recuperated from a relatively routine surgery. As Susie Fulton wrote, "Her term of service in India was short indeed." Full of grief, Fulton wrote that "we cannot understand why one so young, so useful, so eager to serve, and so greatly needed in the mission field should be so suddenly taken away."[8]

Eva May Clements was twenty-three years old. She had been in the mission field for seven months. From the time her call was voted by the General Conference executive committee to the time she was buried was just under ten months.

———

Perhaps some readers, having read this far, may be thinking, *What is the point of this story? What is its significance? What is the catch, the surprise revelation, to justify telling this sad story of a long-forgotten and, on the face of it, unimportant woman? Did she have children who became world-renowned? A cousin who became a division president or a General Conference departmental director? Did a niece, inspired by stories of Aunt Eva, become an immensely successful missionary among an obscure African tribe? Did her staunchness inspire onlookers so much that a local official was converted?*

The answer to each of these questions is No. Eva May Clements had no children and no famous relatives, and her death had an impact on only a small circle of people. She lived in near anonymity, died in obscurity, and rests in a neglected cemetery far from her home, far even from where she had been called to serve and the colleagues who had barely got to know her. Circumstances conspired to consign Eva Clements to oblivion. Her friends and family in Australia grieved when the telegram arrived with the news. But their lives continued. Some three years after her death, a Southern Asia Division committee voted to erect "markers on the graves" of three deceased missionaries; Eva's among them. After that, she was entirely forgotten.[9]

So why do I tell this story? Partly because Eva is not alone in being forgotten. Too often, we only tell the same few stories from Adventist history, the stories of Ellen and James White, Joseph Bates, John Andrews, Uriah Smith, and the first generation of pioneers. To these, we occasionally add the stories of a few famous twentieth-century figures and those considered major church leaders. Yet Adventist history is deep and wide and full of stories we never tell because we do not remember them: extraordinary stories of dedicated men and women who, quite literally, took their lives in their hands but did so because they had put those lives in the hands of the Holy Spirit. As a result, they were willing to risk danger, deprivation, disease, and death.

In many cases, they truly gave their all so that the three angels' messages of Revelation 14 might be proclaimed, the church might be built up, and Jesus lifted up around the world. These ordinary women and men are the makers of the modern, worldwide Seventh-day Adventist Church; yet they are, in many cases, moldering in obscurity. This book tells some of these forgotten stories.

Another reason for starting with Eva's fatal story is because, though it disappeared for so long, it is not entirely lost. Some parts of her story can be recovered. We know little of what she thought or felt, but we can piece together a time line for the last year of her life— something that is impossible for many others. And there were many other missionaries who died in the mission field.

Eva stands for them—and in particular for the many who died, as she did, soon after arriving overseas. We often know little about them other than their sacrifices and their suffering. Eva's experiences can in some sense, represent theirs and remind us that every missionary has a story. No matter how anonymous their deaths, they were wives and daughters, sons and husbands, who were beloved in life and lamented in death.

I also tell this story partly because the tragedy it represents was not uncommon. It is not just Eva's poignant, premature death but its apparent pointlessness that makes it seem so tragic. Eva May Clements never accomplished great deeds for Jesus; she never had the chance. She did her work diligently and cheerfully, but before she could achieve anything noteworthy, she died—willing to give her mortal life in order that others might have eternal life. And in that willingness to serve, to risk literal life and limb, her life was surely not pointless: not in the eyes of her heavenly Father. But also, I hope, not in the eyes of today's Seventh-day Adventist Christians, once we are reminded of these missionaries' stories and their sacrifices.

The stories of Eva and of many others who gave their lives for Adventist mission remind us of the true foundations of the Seventh-day Adventist Church. When established in 1863, it had 3,500 members, found only in the northern states of the United States, plus a handful in Canada. In 2019, Seventh-day Adventist Church members are in almost every country of the world. But today, we can too easily take that outcome for granted because we know how things turned out. It would not have been achieved without God's blessing, but also not without commitment and sacrifice to degrees that are rare today. Past generations of Adventists willingly undertook what the apostle Paul calls Christians' proper service to God—presenting their bodies as living sacrifices.

This short book tells the stories of men and women who are mostly unknown; missionaries who are forgotten, at least by their spiritual (and sometimes literal) descendants—though surely not by our Lord and Savior. Most were very young. Many were women. Many were committed laypeople, and several were self-supporting rather than on the church's payroll.

Simply put, if the Seventh-day Adventist Church had been obliged to rely only on ministers or even just on men, we would not have today's worldwide church. But it didn't. From secretaries to nurses to teachers to builders, church members volunteered, in spite of the risks—as, of course, many young pastors and their families did. But it took the efforts of all, and for many, even the ultimate price was demanded.

In this book, I will stress the sacrifices and commitment of missionaries. I will also highlight the fact that, in our first hundred years, there was rarely a shortage of recruits willing to pay the ultimate price. There is still a worldwide need for service—still areas where the Adventist presence is minimal and tenuous, where missionaries have a vital role to play—and not just in large institutions or organizational administrative headquarters but in "coming close to . . . people by personal effort" as Ellen White memorably puts it.

We still need missionaries. The stories of Eva Clements and other forgotten heroes of the church—the ones who did not become division and General Conference officers and departmental directors but who gave their lives both literally and figuratively—retain, I believe, the power to move us today. I hope that they will encourage old and young to recommit to the prophetic mission of the Seventh-day Adventist Church and inspire members of a new generation to be willing to offer themselves as living sacrifices.

1. "Distribution of Labour," *Australasian Record* 18, no. 41 (October 12, 1914): 18. General Conference Executive Committee, "general Conference Committe Proceedings," General Conference Archives, Silver Spring, MD (hereafter GCA), Record Group 1, vol. XI, pt. ii, 505; news note, *Australasian Record* 24, no. 5 (March 9, 1920): 8.

2. Death notice, *Australasian Record* 24, no. 23 (November 15, 1920): 8; Mrs. J. E. Susan Fulton, "Obituary," *Eastern Tidings* 15, no. 23 (December 1, 1920): 8; Mrs. J. E. Fulton, "Clements," Obituaries, *Australasian Record* 24, no. 26 (December 27, 1920): 7.

3. News note, *Australasian Record*, March 9, 1920, 8; news note, *Eastern Tidings* 15, no. 7 (April 1, 1920): 6; General Conference Executive Committee, meeting of Jan. 5, 1920, p. 505.

4. For John E. Fulton's career, see *The Seventh-day Encyclopedia*, 2nd ed., ed. Don F. Neufeld (Hagerstown, MD: Review and Herald*, 1996), vol. I, p. 577. Eva was always under appointment to serve Fulton, rather than just being called in general to the Southern Asia Division.

5. Fulton, "Clements," 7; Death notice (cited n. 2); 8; extracts from Eva Clement's letters, published as "A Touching Appeal," *Australasian Record*, November 15, 1920, 8.

6. News note, *Eastern Tidings* 15, no. 18 (September 15, 1920): 12; Susan Fulton, letter, September 14, 1920, quoted in *Australasian Record*, November 15, 1920, 7; cf. W. W. Fletcher, "Death of Sister Eva Clements," *Eastern Tidings* 15, no. 22 (November 15, 1920): 8.

7. Fulton, "Obituary," 8.

8. Ibid.

9. "News Notes," *Eastern Tidings* 19, no. 4 (February 15, 1924): 4.

10. Ellen G. White, *The Ministry of Healing* (Mountain View, CA: Pacific Press*, 1937), 143.

CHAPTER 2

The Price to Be Paid

Eric B. Hare in his later years.

In today's world, we tend to have a romanticized view of missionary service. This is partly because our knowledge comes from mission stories, whether those told to camp meeting audiences by returned missionaries, such as Eric B. Hare, or those published as didactic and inspirational short books by Adventist publishing houses in the 1950s, '60s, and '70s, which, like Hare's stories of Dr. Rabbit, were often aimed at children. While many of these stories say something about the risks that missionaries took, they remain upbeat, stressing divine blessings in the face of distress and difficulties, and they often gloss over suffering. Burnished by time and a storyteller's artistry, even disagreeable conditions and deadly dangers could take on a lustrous patina.

This was fine if it inspired Adventists to support foreign missions financially and to serve as cross-cultural missionaries. An unintended consequence, though, is that we in the twenty-first century overlook the dangers of mission service in the nineteenth and early twentieth centuries, when the Seventh-day Adventist Church began to expand worldwide.

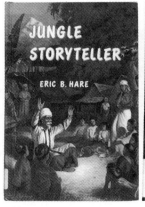

Eric B. Hare books.

This photograph of W. A. Spicer, from the late 1890's, was taken when he was in India, or soon after he became secretary of the Foreign Mission Board.

In 1902, W. A. Spicer, then the secretary of the Foreign Mission Board, explained the situation starkly but candidly: "Those who go into the fields must be ready to lay down their lives, and at the least must be ready to lay everything they have in the world upon the altar of service."[1] In writing thus, Spicer was being neither sentimental nor theoretical. He had been a missionary himself and had suddenly and unexpectedly become superintendent of the India Mission after Dores A. Robinson, the mission superintendent, died of smallpox (a story to which we will return in chapter 7). Spicer knew of what he spoke.

We forget that going as a missionary meant risking one's life. This was true for all missionaries. Most Protestant missionaries in the late 1800s and early 1900s were from Britain and its colonies, continental Europe, and North America.[2] This was true of Seventh-day Adventist missionaries too. Only gradually did a "national" workforce, as Adventists called it (i.e., local workers), emerge in various parts of the world.

W. A. Spicer with Indian pastors and another missionary.

Up until World War II, Adventist mission generally relied on cross-cultural missionaries sent "overseas" from the United States, Great Britain, Germany, and Australia. Indeed, the church's main paper, the *Review and Herald*, for many years published a column every week, variously titled "Missionary Sailings" and "Recent Missionary Departures."

There was, however, one big and often deadly problem: Western-ers lacked resistance to many diseases found in the tropics and sub-tropics, where missionaries were mostly sent.

One modern study shows that the average term of service for the first 214 Protestant missionaries in China in the early and mid-nineteenth century *was just seven years*. The average was so low be-cause roughly one in five missionaries died before serving even seven years.[3] In 1900, there were 17,400 Christian missionaries worldwide. More than 92 percent of missionaries were from Western countries. But only one in six of these was working in Africa because of the high risk of disease and death. "At this stage," one historian writes, "there were still no answers to the killer diseases malaria and sleeping sickness." In West Africa, for example, "The casualty rate among

[Western] missionaries was so high that in the [late] 19th Century they were expected to live just two years."[4]

This poor life expectancy was also true for Seventh-day Adventist missionaries: often they quickly succumbed to and frequently died from a range of tropical and other infectious diseases and fevers. This was the case all around the world, not just in West Africa. The two-year average implies, of course, both shorter and longer life-spans but all clustering around the two-year mark.

Thus, Eva Clements was far from unique in the short period she served as a missionary. Her experience was not only common in terms of Protestant missionaries in general but typical of many early Adventist missionaries, whose deaths all too often cluster around the two-year mark.

In the next chapters, this grim, self-sacrificial reality is illustrated in the stories of missionaries in Africa, Latin America and the Caribbean, the islands of the South Pacific, East Asia, the Middle East, and southern Asia. Many more instances could be added; these are just indicative examples. Often, little is known of these lives that were cut short; ironically, because reports were made from the field to church leaders when a missionary passed away, we know the names of the deceased missionaries and frequently the dates on which they died but often no more than that.

In some cases, however, it has been possible to discover a little more about the lives of these pioneer missionaries, which adds a human face—and sometimes photographs survive so that we do, indeed, know their faces. Occasionally, we also have words written at the time of their deaths, or soon after, by surviving spouses or parents. Twenty-first-century readers may find some of their reports or recollections austere, but people of the late-nineteenth and early twentieth centuries expressed emotion less readily than we do, preferring to retain dignity. It is necessary to read between the lines in order to plumb the depths of emotion underlying their taut, compressed, but undoubtedly distressed reports.

These brief snippets of missionary lives cut short and the expressions of heartache that they evoked exemplify the cost of service. They may lead us to wonder whether the spirit of sacrifice for mission—for entering unentered countries, for reaching unreached and underreached peoples—is still alive. Or is it, like many missionaries in our past, ailing?

1. W. A. Spicer, "The Missionary Campaign," *Review and Herald* 79, no. 37 (September 16, 1902): 24.

2. For example, in China in 1905, "45 per cent of the Protestant missionaries were from Britain and 35 per cent were from America." Marina Xiaojing Wang, "The Evolution of the Ecumenical Vision in the Early Twentieth-Century Chinese Context: A Case Study of the Church of Christ in China (1927–1937)," *Studies in World Christianity* 23, no. 1 (2017): 26.

3. Stephen Neill, *A History of Christian Missions*, 2nd ed. (London: Penguin, 1986), 240.

4. Patrick Johnstone, *The Future of the Global Church: History, Trends and Possibilities* (Downers Grove, IL: IVP Books, 2011), 228, 232, 233, 236.

PART 2
Dying

CHAPTER 3

Facing Deadly Diseases in Africa

O n October 3, 1895, a party of four American missionaries disembarked at the West African port of Cape Coast, in what was then called the Gold Coast, a British colony, today's Ghana. They were not the first Seventh-day Adventists in West Africa; instead, they joined a body of local believers led by Francis Dolphijn, who had been convicted of the seventh-day Sabbath by reading Adventist literature that had, in various ways and for many years, circulated in West Africa. Dolphijn wrote several times to the General Conference, asking it to send missionaries to the Gold Coast.[1]

Cape Coast Ghana c. 1895.

In response came Elder Dudley Hale, accompanied by three other missionaries about whom little is known: G. P. Riggs, a colporteur, and two nurses, George and Eva Kerr, along with the Kerrs' two children. This photograph shows Hale, the Kerrs, and Francis

Front row: George Kerr and Dudley Hale; Back row: Eva Kerr (left) and Francis Dolphijn (center).

Dolphijn. There is no known picture of Riggs. Things did not go well. As a later missionary grimly recorded: "Twenty days had not passed after their arrival before Elder Hale was stricken . . . with the 'black-water' fever." He recovered, but by mid-1896, within eight months of their arrival at Cape Coast in October 1895, both of the Kerrs' children had died, and Riggs had been sent back to England for treatment of dysentery. Despite the treatment, Riggs died in Liverpool on January 8, 1897. The time from his arrival at Cape Coast to his death in Liverpool was just fifteen months.[2]

By the spring, George and Eva Kerr had suffered repeatedly from blackwater fever, and on April 16 they, too, sailed for Liverpool, having served on the Gold Coast for eighteen months. Hale tried to carry on, writing

Dudley Hale.

William H. Anderson (known as Harry) and his wife Nora.

forlornly, "I am left alone with the work here." In fact, he had Dolphijn and other local believers. Hale, however, was suffering from chronic severe malaria; on June 3, 1897, he sailed for England. He had been a missionary for twenty-one months. Three of the original party perished, and none of the other three lasted even two years. Hale recovered his health and served briefly in the Caribbean (as we will see in chapter 4), returned to the Gold Coast early in 1903, "but was again forced by malaria to leave almost immediately." Still, he survived.[3]

Meanwhile, on July 5, 1894, a party of seven Seventh-day Adventist missionaries had arrived in Bulawayo, new capital of the newest part of the British Empire, Rhodesia, which had been conquered from the indigenous inhabitants, the Ndebele, who the British called Matabele. Rhodesia was vast, covering what today are the nations of Zambia and Zimbabwe. The Adventists established a mission station at Solusi, in Matabeleland, in present-day Zimbabwe. Most returned soon after to South Africa, leaving a South African layman, Fred Sparrow, in charge of the property. In July 1895, a second party of missionaries arrived after a long wagon journey across Bechuanaland (today's Botswana). It included Elder George B. Tripp, who became the first superintendent of the Solusi Mission, his wife, Mary, and twelve-year-old, George Junior. Mary had married George Senior that March, immediately before departing America for South Africa. As we will see, many missionaries married right before leaving for foreign service. Other American missionaries in the 1895 party included Elder William H. Anderson (known as Harry) and his wife Nora, pictured on this page, both of whom were fresh out of college; and a sixty-year-old medical missionary, Dr. A. S. Carmichael. There were also South Africans: Fred Sparrow, his brother, Chris, and Chris's wife, Mahalah, who helped manage the mission farm. A photograph survives of Chris Sparrow: he is pictured with some of the local farm laborers and their families.

In 1897, another American missionary family reached Solusi: Frank B. Armitage, his wife, Anna, and their ten-year-old daughter, Violet, who had journeyed by donkey cart. However, by the end of the year, the railroad had reached Bulawayo, and in January 1898

the president of the General Conference, Ole Olsen, visited Solusi, traveling most of the way by train. When the Armitages made their more arduous journey, Frank was thirty-two and Annie thirty-eight; they had then been married thirteen years but would not make it to fourteen. In 1898, as Harry Anderson wrote to church leaders, "quite an epidemic, almost a plague" of malaria swept across Rhodesia. According to his report, people were "dying everywhere. In Buluwayo [sic] the hospital is full, and the doctor said he did not believe there was a well man in the town." Solusi was not spared.[4]

Chris Sparrow is pictured with some of Solusi Mission's local farm laborers and their families.

GEORGE BYRON TRIPP JR
DIED APRIL 5, 1898.
AGE 12 YEARS.
"A YOUTHFUL SACRIFICE"

The graves and the cemetery at Solusi where father and son and many other missionaries still lie.

Dr. Carmichael contracted malaria on February 14; two weeks later he died. Elder Tripp conducted the funeral and the next day collapsed. On March 7, he died and was buried. He had served at the mission "just three years." Also on March 7, Chris Sparrow's young daughter, whose name is not known, died. Her mother, Mahalah, survived, but later was "laid to rest by the side of her daughter in the cemetery at Solusi." On April 5 , George Tripp Jr. died and was buried next to his father. Nora Anderson, the widowed Mary Tripp, and the three members of the Armitage family were suffering badly with fever, and all were sent by train to Cape Town. Annie Armitage never reached it; she was so ill that she was forced to stop in Kimberly, where she passed away, having served as a missionary for less than a year. Eventually, Frank Armitage and Mary Tripp, widower and widow, found consolation in each other and in 1899 were married; they returned to serve at Solusi. Harry and Nora Anderson were reunited and raised a daughter, Naomi, at Solusi. But the cemetery at Solusi remains a silent and potent witness to the mortality rate of mission in Matabeleland.[5]

Solusi cemetery.

Later, a South African Adventist poetess memorialized what she dubbed "Solusi's Silent Village," which evokes the spirit of sacrifice that gave rise to today's hundreds of thousands of Zambian and Zimbabwean Seventh-day Adventists:

In Solusi's silent village

The four-o'clocks now bloom
They cover up the hardness;
They make a cozy room.
. . .
A son and father rest there,
The dates two months apart.
A mother lies near daughter,
As tho' still of one heart.
Some large trees stand on guard there
Inside the sheltering fence.
The sleeping ones are waiting
For Christ to call them hence.[6]

Anderson, who was for a time the sole American left at Solusi, wrote a report for the church paper in America in which he stressed that the epidemic had carried off not missionaries alone but also many local believers. It was they about whom he was most concerned, not merely their mortal lives, but their eternal futures:

O for men and women to give their lives, if need be, for this people! We need young men and women,—those who can stand the change of climate, who can easily acquire the language, who are strong in faith, and who do not easily yield to discouragement. We need those who are willing to leave their country, kindred, and homes, to lead, others to the promised land.[7]

———

God's cause had to be upheld in other parts of Africa, too, of course; and in other parts of Africa, too, missionaries faced their mortality. In 1903, the German Union Conference took a bold (and expensive) step in establishing a new mission in what was then German East Africa (today part of the country of Tanzania). This was a rousing step for Adventists in Germany, as the church in their country committed to foreign mission. Among those moved to serve was Christian Wunderlich, a layman and skilled craftsman in his fifties. On February 20, 1904, he sailed from Hamburg on the steamship

Kaiser, part of a group of missionaries and "the second party to German East Africa." On arrival at the Pare Mission, Christian assisted in construction "of the mission buildings" and with running a steam traction engine. Sometime in 1905, Christian and a missionary couple were "stricken" with an unknown but serious illness. They "returned to . . . Germany," where the husband and wife survived their illness, but Christian's turned out "to [be] a fatal sickness."[8]

He was treated at Friedensau Sanitarium and declared his intention of returning to Pare. Going back to Africa was, a colleague wrote, "his chief concern, even during his illness, as his whole soul had been stirred by the needs of the African peoples." Christian's wish was not to be granted, though, for he died on October 31, 1905. He was the first missionary to German East Africa to die. Christian Wunderlich was buried in the

Christian Wunderlich's "neat little tombstone."

cemetery at Friedensau, near the "mission school"; according to the president of the German Union, L. R. Conradi, "His neat little tombstone" was meant to "remind our students of the spirit that it takes to build up missions" and move them "to devote their lives to the noble work of the self-denying missionary." Whatever his legacy, Wunderlich had, as his obituary observes, "spent less than two years in Africa."[9]

East Africa, however, was not as lethal as West Africa, with which we began this chapter. After the debacles in 1895–1897 and 1903, the church found a missionary who had staying power and could provide lasting leadership, including to the indigenous Adventists who continued to witness. In 1905, two years after Dudley Hale was for the second time forced to leave West Africa by illness, David C. Babcock, his third wife, Wilhelmina, and their children arrived in Sierra Leone. Babcock had served for five years in the West Indies, where his second wife, Elmira, had died (discussed in chapter 4).

He was to work in West Africa for the next twelve years.[10]

David Babcock laid strong foundations for later missional success; the largest Adventist university in West Africa, Babcock University in Nigeria, is named after him. At the time, however, that was truly unforeseeable as he strove to make the most of limited resources and difficult circumstances. For most Westerners, conditions on "the west coast of Africa, known as the 'white man's grave,' " as one General Conference vice president put it, were terribly taxing. Indeed, in 1911, Babcock developed a plan, approved by church leaders, for "establishing a recuperating-station" in the

David and Mina Babcock, portrait probably taken in Freetown, Sierra Leone.

David C. Babcock, pioneer missionary.

Canary Islands for missionaries "when they need rest from the work and trying climate."[11]

The Gold Coast, which had undone Riggs and the Kerrs in 1895–96, was seen as especially unhealthy for Westerners; even nearly twenty years later its name evoked dread when missionaries elsewhere in West Africa were asked to serve there. Adventist missionaries to the Gold Coast were regularly evacuated temporarily to Freetown for treatment of fevers; not all missionaries to West Africa died, but most were seriously ill several times. Freetown, in Sierra Leone, was not itself the healthiest locale for missionaries but, as a large port-city, it had better medical facilities than existed in Ghana at this point and this was one reason Babcock made it the headquarters of the West African Mission.[12]

In May 1908, two new missionaries accepted a call to serve in Sierra Leone. Thomas and Katherine French, both teachers, arrived in Freetown in August 1908. Both suffered from malaria while in Sierra Leone but survived for two and a half years, during which they both taught at church schools, while Thomas also pastored the Freetown church and trained nationals to serve as missionaries elsewhere in West Africa. Late in 1910, they were asked to move to the Gold Coast and to Axim, site of a mission school, where they arrived soon after New Year, 1911. They had been there just a few days when on January 17, 1911, Katherine "was taken ill with a severe attack of blackwater fever," as Thomas described it in her obituary. She lived only one day, dying of heart failure on January 18, 1911.[13]

In writing of Katherine's passing, Thomas articulates the bewilderment, the distress, and yet the determination typical of many Adventist missionaries confronting the death of a loved one:

> . . . as I stood beside my dying companion a few days ago, and realized that my own strength was fast failing, in my perplexity my mind turned to my brethren and sisters at home, who have so nobly supported this cause by their prayers and by their means; and the thought came to me, "Have they let go the hands?" And again . . . the question came forcibly to me, "What can this crisis mean? Have our dear people forgotten to hold up the hands over the armies of Israel?"
>
> We appeal to our people at home to . . . support the languishing hands of our workers in . . . in these heathen strongholds. Brethren and sisters, seek God earnestly in behalf of his cause in West Africa.[14]

A deceased spouse's survivor sometimes suffered from the same illness, and certainly they did not swiftly recover from the emotional impact of a loved one's death. A colleague wrote of how "Elder French was greatly reduced in vitality" as a result of "overwork, and the sad experience he was called to go through." Exhausted mentally, spiritually, and physically, French left the Gold Coast in February, "to return home to regain his health."[15]

To replace Katherine and Thomas French at Axim, two lay missionaries, C. E. F. Thompson and his wife (whose name is unknown) were called. We know little of Thompson, but he was Jamaican, well educated, a skillful writer—and, as a studio photograph shows, a stylish dresser![16] Using a West Indian missionary in West Africa probably reflected a belief, then widespread in Europe and North America (but now discredited), that people of the Caribbean, descended from slaves taken from Central and West Africa, had natural resistance to diseases endemic in the tropical regions on both sides of the Atlantic.[17] Thompson had served in Sierra Leone in 1908 before being sent to Axim in the Gold Coast Colony in

C. E. F. Thompson, first Jamaican Adventist missionary

early 1909; he helped to found and taught in Adventist schools in both countries and, though not ordained, was a successful soul-winner. He is pictured here with three Ghanaian converts, members of the Nsymba church, and David Babcock, photographed in October 1909 when Babcock visited the Gold Coast.[18]

Twelve months later, Thompson was back in Sierra Leone, supervising mission work on the island of Sherbro, where an Adventist presence had been established only in February 1910. Clearly, Thompson was a trusted worker—and this is evident, too, in the fact that only a few months later he was sent back to Axim, an important mission outpost, following the departure of the grieving and shattered Thomas French.[19]

In less than a year after Thompson's return to Axim, he won some thirty converts. Given his track record, it seems likely that the reason he was not ordained was, simply, that he was, in the language of the time, "colored" and missionaries were supposed to be white. Thompson's race is thus likely to have shaped his whole, short missionary career. But being black did not stop him from contracting Bright's disease. He went to Sierra Leone to seek treatment for his failing kidneys, but to no avail. Having served in West Africa for fewer than four years, C. E. F. Thompson died in Freetown on March 25, 1912, leaving his wife a widow.[20]

Back in southern Africa, missionaries and their children still passed away at Solusi, but less frequently than before.[21] Meanwhile, other mission stations also claimed lives. The story of the Konigmacher family, who went to what was then Nyasaland, will be told in chapter 12. To the south and west, Mary Cobban served in South Africa and Rhodesia. She had been baptized as a girl by Elder George Tripp, before he left the United States for Solusi. A school teacher, on December 18, 1908, having recently turned twenty-four, she accepted a call to South Africa to teach at Claremont College. Later she taught at Solusi. While a missionary in Rhodesia, she married

C. E. F. Thompson, David Babcock, and members of the Nsymba church in October 1909, when Babcock visited the Gold Coast.

one Arthur Ingle. Late in 1913, she contracted an unknown fever; after an illness of three months, she died in Durban, South Africa, on March 8, 1914, at the age of thirty.[22]

Meanwhile, in April 1912, the thirty-one-year-old Charles Lindsay Bowen, known as Lynn, sailed for South Africa with his wife, Ida, who was thirty-five, and their younger daughter, Ethel, six; their older daughter, Louise, remained in the United States under the care of her grandmother. The Bowens took up station in Rhodesia: in their case, at Tsungwesi Mission in Manicaland, which like Solusi is in today's Zimbabwe, but to the east of Matabeleland. At some point in 1912, Ida gave birth to a son, Laurence. A contemporary photo shows that Lynn was a handsome young man; in his hometown he was remembered as "a young man of pronounced personality, an earnest Christian and one who made lasting friends wherever he was known." In 1913 there was an outbreak of smallpox at Tsungwesi, and Lynn and his two children contracted the disease. Chris Sparrow arrived and helped Ida treat the others at the mission suffering with smallpox, Ethel and Laurence among them. It was too late, though, for Lynn Bowen, who suffered for three weeks. As Ida later wrote to Lynn's uncle, "He had complications which made it very difficult and painful for him to breathe and swallow." Sparrow later reported that Ethel had recovered but that little Laurence "was at his worst at the time of his father's death." Later, "the little boy . . . also recovered," so that all the family members were well.[23]

Charles Lindsay Bowen

Ida Nelson Bowen.

All the family, that is, except for the husband and father. Sparrow's arrival and nursing came too late. In his report to church leaders, Sparrow describes Lynn's three-weeks' suffering in grueling detail and records Bowen's final, painful, prayer "that if it was the Lord's will for him to recover it might be speedily; if not, that the Lord might release him from the agony he was in."[24]

On June 2, 1913, Lynn died, aged thirty-two, at the mission where he had served for only a year. Just over four years later, Ida and Ethel, who had remained in Africa, were forced to watch as Laurence, who had grown up not knowing his father, died of dysentery.[25] Meanwhile, news of Lynn's passing had been received at the 1913 General Conference Session the very day after he died. Ida, who had been forced to witness his suffering, sent a telegram to the United States with the simple but profoundly sad message: "My husband died yesterday at 1 P.M."[26]

---

1. *The Seventh-day Adventist Encyclopedia*, 2nd ed., ed. Don F. Neufeld (Hagerstown, MD: Review and Herald®, 1996), vol. I, s.v. "Ghana."

2. Ibid. William H. Lewis, "True Adventures in Africa: A Story of the Pioneer Days of the Advent Movement in Sierra Leone and Ghana West Africa" (unpublished manuscript, 1971), GCA, Record Group 509, box 12983, p. 17. William H. Lewis did not arrive in the Gold Coast until more than a decade later, but he knew the African believers and learned of the events from them.

3. D. U. Hale, "Cape Coast, West Africa," *Review and Herald* 74, no. 26 (June 29, 1897): 408; *Seventh-day Adventist Encyclopedia*, s.v. "Hale, Dudley Upton."

4. Jean Cripps, "Our History—6: Moon Eclipse Triggers Rebellion," *Trans-Africa Division Outlook* 69, no. 4 (April 15, 1971): 8; "Armitage," Obituaries, *Review and Herald* 129, no. 17 (April 24, 1952): 20; W. H. Anderson, "Africa," Letters, *Missionary Magazine* 10, no. 7 (July 1898): 263.

5. Cripps, "Our History," p. 8; W. H. Anderson, W. S. Hyatt, and J. M. Freeman, "Africa," Letters, *Missionary Magazine* 10, no. 7 (July 1898): 263–265; "Armitage," 20; W. C. Tarr, "The Battle of the Early Days," *Southern African Division Outlook* 42, no. 11 (July 17, 1944): 2.

6. Mrs. W. R. Vail, "Solusi's 'Silent Village,' " *South African Division Outlook*, July 17, 1942, 4.

7. W. H. Anderson, "Matabeleland," *Review and Herald* 75, no. 23 (June 7, 1898): 368.

8. W. A. S[picer], "The Price of Victory," *Review and Herald* 83, no. 3 (January 18, 1906): 5; L. R. Conradi, "Missions in German East Africa," *Review and Herald* 83, no. 24 (June 14, 1906): 13; *Hamburg Passenger Lists, 1850–1934* (Provo, UT: Ancestry.com, 2008), online database.

9. Untitled obituary, *Review and Herald* 82, no. 47 (November 23, 1905): 24; Conradi, "Missions in German East Africa," 14; L. R. Conradi, "Progress of the Work in the German Union Conference," *Review and Herald* 83, no. 44 (November 1, 1906): 14.

10. I. H. Evans, "Elder D. C. Babcock," Obituaries, *Review and Herald* 109, no. 18 (May 5, 1932): 430.

11. Ibid.; 430; D. C. Babcock, "West Africa," *Review and Herald* 88, no. 51 (December 21, 1911): 13; cf. Lewis, "True Adventures in Africa," 19.

12. Lewis, "True Adventures in Africa," 18, 19; see also 6, 20, 23. D. C. Babcock, "The Work in West Africa," *Review and Herald* 86, no. 26 (July 1, 1909): 15; D. C. Babcock, "West Africa," 13, 14.

13. T. M. French, "French," Obituaries, *Review and Herald* 88, no. 13 (March 30, 1911): 23. The facts of the Frenches' time in Sierra Leone are from D. C. Babcock, "West Africa," *Review and Herald* 85, no. 52 (December 24, 1908): 19; Babcock, "The Work in West Africa," 15; D. C. Babcock, quoted in "Other Mission Fields," in *The Story of Our Missions for 1909*, special issue, *Review and Herald* 87, no. 24 (June 16, 1910): 61; Mrs. D. C. Babcock, "Workers' Meeting in West Africa," *Review and Herald* 88, no. 5 (February 2, 1911): 9, 10.

14. T. M. French, "West Africa's Appeal," *Review and Herald* 88, no. 13 (March 30, 1911): 10.

15. Babcock, "West Africa," December 21, 1911, 13; untitled news note, *Review and Herald* 88, no. 13 (March 30, 1911): 24.

16. D. C. Babcock, "Thompson," Obituaries, *Review and Herald* 89, no. 21 (May 23, 1912): 23; C. E. F. Thompson, "West Coast, Africa," *Review and Herald* 85, no. 36 (September 3, 1908): 18. Babcock mentions Thompson's literary ability in his obituary, and it is evident in the article by Thompson.

17. Mariola Espinosa, "The Question of Racial Immunity to Yellow Fever in History and Historiography," *Social Science History* 38, (Fall/Winter 2014): 437–453.

18. D. C. Babcock, "West Africa," *Review and Herald* 87, no. 2 (January 13, 1910): 13. See T. M. French, "West Africa," *Review and Herald* 86, no. 39 (September 30, 1909): 13; Babcock,

"Other Mission Fields," 60; Mrs. Babcock, "Workers' Meeting," 9.

19. See Mrs. Babcock, "Workers' Meeting," 9; Babcock, "West Africa," December 21, 1911, 13; D. C. Babcock, "Sherbro, West Africa," *Review and Herald* 87, no. 26 (June 30, 1910): 9.

20. Babcock, "Thompson," 23; untitled news notes, *Review and Herald* 89, no. 18 (May 2, 1912): 24; D. C. Babcock, "West African Mission," *General Conference Bulletin* 7, no. 18 (June 5, 1913): 277.

21. Tarr, "The Battle of the Early Days," 2.

22. A. G. Daniells, "Mary Isabelle Cobban-Ingle," Obituaries, *Review and Herald* 91, no. 25 (June 18, 1914): 21.

23. "Missionary C. L. Bowen Is Dead in Africa," *Randolph (NY) Register*, June 6, 1913, 2. T. E. Bowen, "Another Life for Africa," *Review and Herald* 90, no. 34 (August 21, 1913): 804. C. R. Sparrow, "Tsungwesi Mission," *South African Missionary* 12, no. 30 (August 18, 1913): 3.

24. Sparrow, "Tsungwesi Mission," 3.

25. Untitled news note, *Review and Herald* 95, no. 5 (January 31, 1918): 24.

26. Bowen, "Another Life for Africa," 804.

CHAPTER 4

Dying in the Americas

dventist pioneers risked death not just in not Africa but in the
Americas too. While the islands and coastal regions of the
Caribbean were close to the United States—in the same hemisphere as the church's homeland—they were also home to many virulent
diseases, such as yellow fever, "that dread scourge of the tropics of the
western hemisphere," as an Adventist church leader wrote grimly.[1]
Debilitating illnesses and untimely deaths were the prices to be paid
for evangelizing the Inter-American region.

As in West Africa, Seventh-day Adventist missionaries to the West
Indies were not the first seventh-day Sabbath keepers in the region.
An Adventist presence in the Caribbean developed early, thanks partly
to pamphlets sent to the islands by the International Tract Society
and partly to American colporteurs (literature evangelists) who traveled through the islands, selling Adventist books and pamphlets.
These colporteurs were laypeople who supported themselves through
their sales, and so they stayed in a place for only a short time before
moving on, seeking fresh markets. Missionaries who would stay and
ministers were needed to build on these foundations.

On November 20, 1890, Dexter A. Ball and his wife, Martha, and
their young daughter, Myrtle, disembarked in Bridgetown, Barbados,
which was then a British colony. They were the first official Adventist
missionaries to an island in the Lesser Antilles. The Balls settled in
Bridgetown, and Dexter and Martha began to work. In September
1891, the first Seventh-day Adventist church on the island was organized (see photography, p. 46), but Dexter's serious illness forced
the Balls to retreat to the United States the following year. They had
not been on the island even two years; returning to the States spared
their lives, but this pattern of missionary sickness, suffering, and often
death was to be repeated again and again.[2]

Dexter, Martha, and Myrtle Ball (at left)

Several of Pastor Ball's converts became lay missionaries to the other islands of the eastern Caribbean. One of them, Charles Adamson, at the request of church leaders, went to work in Trinidad as a self-supporting colporteur-evangelist. This Barbadian was the first missionary to the islands of Trinidad and Tobago, where he had a degree of success. As a result, there was a request to send an ordained minister to Trinidad. There may have been a lack of volunteers because, in the end, the Foreign Mission Board called a ministerial licentiate, Andrew E. Flowers, who was then ordained and sent to Trinidad. He and his wife, Rachael, landed in Port of Spain, the capital of Trinidad and Tobago, in February 1894. Flowers had received his ministerial license in 1891, but he had been a colporteur for many years, in addition to his

Bridgetown, Barbados: the first Seventh-day Adventist Church.

three years of pastoral-evangelistic experience. Rachael had been involved in literature evangelism herself and actively supported Andrew's ministry. As a colleague later recalled, Andrew Flowers was a pleasant and kindly man, "beloved by all who knew him"—important characteristics for a missionary.[3]

Andrew and Rachael started working enthusiastically but faced considerable hostility in Port of Spain. They switched their focus to Couva, which is on the western coast of Trinidad, where they "found a few believers already rejoicing in the truth," due to the efforts of Adamson and other colporteurs. Soon twenty to twenty-five people were regularly attending Sabbath services, and the first Seventh-day Adventist church in Trinidad would later be organized in Couva.

Sadly, Andrew Flowers did not live to see the fruits of his labors. As another missionary to the eastern Caribbean recalled, he was "stricken with that dread disease of the tropics, yellow fever, or 'yellow jack,' as it is termed locally." He suffered for five days. According to an eyewitness to his suffering, "As he began to realize that his end was near, he said it was 'all right.' " With this remarkable statement of faith, Andrew Flowers passed away on July 29, 1894.[4]

Couva, Trinidad.

For Rachael, herself "stricken" with illness, the news of her husband's death came like a "blow . . . with dreadful force," as a sympathetic observer noted. She was "prostrate with the fever, and unable to attend her husband's funeral" and returned to the United States soon after. Yet she was not disillusioned; instead, she urged that more workers be sent to Trinidad. The following year she went to Guadalajara, Mexico, where she served as a missionary for two years. "Feeling a great burden for the work . . . in the islands, and her health being somewhat improved, she returned to Trinidad." It is at this point that her story intertwines with that of another missionary family.[5]

In August 1895, a year after Andrew Flowers passed away, a replacement minister, Edwin W. Webster, arrived in Trinidad with his wife, Lucy, and daughter, Mabel. Edwin, thirty-three years old, and Lucy, twenty-five, worked as a team: he conducted evangelism and Bible studies, she created thriving Sabbath Schools for children, and together they cowrote some reports from the island. After seventeen months, on January 15, 1897, Edwin "had the satisfaction of dedicating the Couva church, the first Seventh-day Adventist church building in Trinidad."(shown on p. 48)[6]

Ten months later, however, all three Websters contracted yellow fever. Lucy died in late November 1897, followed by Mabel in late

December. Because of the fear of contagion, Edwin could find no one willing to help him bury her. As George Enoch, a fellow missionary to the West Indies, sadly recorded, "Little Mabel . . . was put into her coffin and carried . . . by her own bereaved father," who was still ill himself but "had survived and was recovered sufficiently to do what money could not hire others to do."[7] Lucy spent two years and three months in mission service before it killed her.

Remarkably, a year later, Rachael Flowers and Edwin Webster were married. Having each lost a spouse to diseases in the Caribbean, they found consolation in each other. Edwin and Rachael then served in Trinidad until July 1900; at that point, "on account of the impaired health of both of them, Brother and Sister Webster returned to the States, locating in different places that seemed to give the most hope for the recovery of their health."[8]

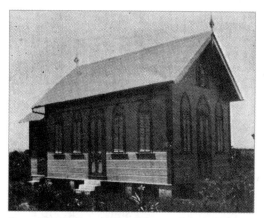

Couva, Trinidad, Seventh-day Adventist Church.

In February 1900, David C. Babcock (who had already been widowed once) arrived with his second wife, Elmira, in Georgetown, British Guiana (now Guyana); they were both forty-five years old. Elmira suffered from illnesses for much of their time in British Guiana, but as fellow missionary Albert J. Haysmer reported, "She desired to remain at their post of duty, as they felt that no change could avert the sad result." Elmira died on June 20, 1901, after just sixteen months' service.[9]

Babcock had initially been called in 1899 to lead the mission in Trinidad, but another missionary—the unfortunate Dudley Hale—left British Guiana hastily because his wife was ill, and he feared for her life. Babcock was therefore reassigned to British Guiana, and Luther Crowther was called to serve in Trinidad in December 1899. The Dakota Conference, where Crowther had been pastoring, continued to contribute to his salary. By April 1900, Luther and Laura Crowther, forty-two and forty years of age respectively; their son, Raymond, who was fifteen; and daughter, Alpha, thirteen, had begun to settle into life in Port of Spain, despite the loss of some of their belongings when a Dutch ship transporting them sank.

For sixteen months, Crowther worked diligently and successfully in Trinidad. In a letter to former colleagues in the Dakota Conference, he vividly described his mission field in terms they could appreciate: "There is more vice, profanity, drunkenness, and general degradation within a block of our mission than you could easily gather together in all Sioux Falls. More fights and arrests occur before our hall than in any ward of your city, to say the least. . . . Yet our people live in the midst of this, and live as close to the Lord as many in America. The truth has power to keep from sin, if we only receive it."[10]

On Sabbath, August 13, 1901, Luther spoke during Sabbath School but, as Laura later wrote to a friend, "he . . . had to leave before it closed. He took his bed, and never got up again." He was seen by a doctor and two "trained nurses," who variously diagnosed "jungle fever" and "pernicious malarial fever." Whatever exactly ailed Luther, it was lethal. He "was sick one week." Luther M. Crowther passed away on August 25, 1901, having served as a missionary for well under two years.[11]

Laura had to make arrangements first for the funeral and then for her return with her children to the United States. She also wrote the obituary notice for her husband, which was published in the *Review and Herald*; its formal, Victorian language hints at heartbreak: "We have laid him to rest till Jesus comes. He leaves a wife, one son, and one daughter."[12]

Around this time, Albert and Ida Fischer were called to the recently acquired American territory of Puerto Rico "to open up the work." They disembarked there in late May 1901. Less than nine months later, both became seriously ill. After an illness of thirty-five days, during which he suffered "four or five severe hemorrhages," Fischer died of typhoid fever in Mayagüez on March 23, 1902. He was thirty years old.

Albert Haysmer, a fellow missionary to the Caribbean who helped to nurse Fischer on his deathbed, hints of the grief felt by the widow who had survived her fever: "She knows that the Lord has made no mistake, although she cannot now see why this blow has come." But his report dwelt on Albert Fischer: "He was . . . afraid that many would think that he and his wife had made a mistake in coming to this field. He wished me to express his strong belief that the Lord had sent them, and to state that they did not regret the move they had taken, but that, if the Lord should call him aside to rest awhile, he was glad to be found at his post of duty." Haysmer concluded his report of Fischer's death as follows: "Who will step in and carry on the work begun?"[13]

In 1905, Charles W. Enoch, a nurse and masseur who had worked at the Portland Sanitarium and spent a year in literature evangelism, and his wife, also a nurse, went to the West Indies as medical missionaries. (Her name is unknown since in contemporary sources she is always referred to, and even refers to herself, as Mrs. C. W. Enoch; they had one child, whose name is likewise unknown.) The Enoch family landed in Barbados in November 1905 and opened "treatment rooms" in Bridgetown that were advertised as follows: "Treatments along rational lines in strict conformity to the Battle Creek system are given." This was the first medical missionary work in the West Indies. Enoch also took on the double roles of secretary and treasurer of the East Caribbean Conference, which took him to other islands. The Barbados Treatment Rooms met with considerable initial success and continued to operate throughout 1906.[14]

At the end of the year, however, Mr. and Mrs. C. W. Enoch sailed from Bridgetown to Port of Spain, Trinidad, which lay in the South Caribbean Conference. They may have moved because the treatment rooms had, despite initial high hopes, proven not to be financially viable: another missionary recorded, "Much good was accomplished" in Bridgetown by Enoch, but "it was thought best to move the work to Port of Spain," which hints at some difficulties.[15]

However, Charles's brother George, who had been a missionary in Trinidad since 1901, was called at the 1906 Annual Council to serve in India. George sailed from Port of Spain just after Charles and his wife landed there on New Year's Day 1907. Perhaps Charles wanted to continue his brother's ministry.

In any case, upon arriving, Charles and his wife promptly opened a new treatment room, in which, according to an advertisement, "Dyspepsia, Rheumatism, Fevers, and kindred ailments, are successfully treated." The treatment rooms immediately attracted wealthy customers, but, as events proved, the Enochs were not able to "successfully treat" the most feared kind of fever. Charles contracted yellow fever on February 1, 1907, suffered from the intense symptoms of this virulent disease, and died on February 5.[16]

He had been in Trinidad for one month and in the Caribbean for a little over fourteen months.

His wife continued to operate the treatment rooms in Port of Spain through the end of February but not after that. It seems likely that she, too, may have passed away in Trinidad. Sterrie A. Wellman, a missionary leader in the West Indies, had reported to the General Conference secretary soon after Charles's death that "his wife, though sick and broken with the shock, is of good courage in the Lord, and earnestly desires that the work begun should be carried forward by others."[17] Her fate and that of their child remain unknown.

As colleagues commented at the time, Charles Enoch had been an active worker; even ten months later, West Indian church members commented on their "sense of loss in being deprived of his faithful labors." Ovid E. Davis, who had succeeded Babcock in 1906 as the superintendent of the nearby Guiana Mission (and died in 1911 while pioneering in the remote, mountainous jungle around Mount Roraima on the Guyana-Venezuela border), wrote grimly of how three church workers had been "laid away in Port of Spain. But the message must be given and who will volunteer to aid in this work?"[18]

George Enoch, reacting to the bad news, seemed almost upbeat about his brother's fate. In a letter to William Spicer, the General Conference secretary, George echoes Haysmer's comments about Fischer five years earlier: "I am thankful that he died at his post of duty. . . . We have no regrets to offer, but . . . bind our lives on the altar of missionary endeavor." George raises his late brother's past only in connection with a possible future: "The last thought of such a falling worker is not of regret at having made the effort, but rather, Will some one grasp the standard as it falls from my hands?" While acknowledging that their "hearts . . . bowed in sadness," his real concern is clear when writing of how "the thought presses heavily upon us, will this branch of the work in the West Indies, which we strove together so hard to get upon its feet, be now left to languish for the lack of consecrated workers?" Again and again, missionaries cared as much for the future of the work as for themselves or their deceased friends and family.[19]

Soon after this, a fourth missionary died in Trinidad: again, a young man who left both a widow and a young child. In 1907, when twenty-three years old and belatedly completing his high-school education at South Lancaster Academy, Robert L. Price was called to the Caribbean to replace George Enoch in the Watchman Publishing House in Trinidad. Robert and his wife, Sarah Bessie (who went by Bessie), accepted the call. In September 1907, shortly after their son, Robert Jr., celebrated his second birthday, the young family sailed from New York to Port of Spain.

Price did "able and efficient work" in the publishing house as well as serving as the South Caribbean Conference secretary. But on May 26, he "was stricken with fever." Four doctors attended him, but like Charles Enoch, his illness was a short one, and "he passed this life on . . . May 31." Although "delirious with pain for the last thirty-six hours he was conscious at intervals and an hour before he died" he asked the Adventists around his bed "to sing to him . . . 'Jesus, Lover of my Soul.' He also asked for prayer" and soon after "went to sleep." Robert Price was buried alongside Enoch and the two other Adventist missionaries; all four had died of tropical diseases.[20] Price had been a missionary in Trinidad for not quite eight months.

Charles Enoch and Robert Price were not the last missionaries to die soon after arriving in Port of Spain. On October 27, 1918, a family landed in Trinidad: Charles B. Sutton, who had just turned thirty-six; his wife, Dottie, aged twenty-nine; and their daughter, Eleanor, had just turned seven. Charles had worked in the publishing department of the Kansas Conference, where he and Dottie had been married in 1911. In January 1918, he had been called to the South Caribbean Conference. His employers in Kansas claimed they could not replace him and managed to have his call temporarily suspended in May. But by July the need of the mission field had been given precedence. At the end of August, Sutton applied for his first American passport for himself, his wife, and his daughter. They sailed from New Orleans, which must have seemed extraordinary and exotic to a family that had never been outside Kansas before

Charles B. Sutton and his wife, Dottie, at the time of their wedding.

their journey to the mission field—a trip they surely started full of hope and expectation. Dottie fell ill during the voyage, and the day after they disembarked, she died. She survived in the mission field less than forty-eight hours.[21]

Meanwhile, the death toll of missionaries to South America was not as great as in Central America and the West Indies. This was due in part because Adventists mostly worked in the temperate and long-settled regions of Argentina and Brazil during the early years of mission work on the continent, and these regions had life expectancies similar to Europe. But nothing could be taken for granted, as the Haak family discovered. On February 5, 1914, Bruno Carl Haak, a young German American, applied for passports for himself; his wife, Elva Mae; and their two children, Raymond and Ardice. Later that month, the Haaks sailed from New York City, first to Liverpool, and then after an eight-day break in England, on to Buenos Aires, Argentina. They landed there on March 24, 1914.[22]

Bruno was just twenty-nine years old but was soon elected president of the Argentine Conference. He worked energetically among Argentina's large German-speaking community—but not for long. On November 25, 1914, Bruno C. Haak died of typhoid fever. His fellow missionary J. W. Westphal reported, "For nearly a week before his demise he was delirious," hinting of the horrors of death by typhoid a hundred years ago. Westphal added that Haak left "a much-loved companion and two children to mourn, the latter being too young to realize their loss." In fact, Raymond was five, and Ardice not quite three. Their mother, Elva, now a widow, was twenty-eight. As for Bruno himself, he died eleven weeks past his thirtieth birthday. His career as a missionary had lasted eight months.[23]

---

1. G. C. T[enney], "Death of Elder A. E. Flowers," Obituary Notices, *Review and Herald* 71, no. 34 (August 21, 1894): 544.

2. See Glenn O. Phillips, *Over a Century of Adventism, 1884–1991* (Barbados: East Caribbean Conference of Seventh-day Adventists, 1991).

3. *The Seventh-day Encyclopedia*, 2nd ed., ed. Don F. Neufeld (Hagerstown, MD: Review and Herald®, 1996), *Seventh-day Adventists in Barbados*: vol. 2, s.v. "Trinidad and Tobago." Tenney, "Death of Elder A. E. Flowers," 544. See George F. Enoch, *Glimpses of the Caribbean: The Advent Message in the Sunny Caribbean* (Port of Spain, Trinidad and Tobago: West Indian Union Conference of Seventh-day Adventists, 1907), 16, 17; W. S. Hyatt, "Flowers," Obituary Notices, *Review and Herald* 71, no. 46 (November 20, 1894): 735; Smith Sharp, "Mrs. E. W. Webster," Obituaries, *Review and Herald* 89, no. 25 (June 20, 1912): 22; General Conference of Seventh-day Adventists, *Seventh-day Adventist Year Book, 1886* (Battle Creek, MI: Seventh-

day Adventist Pub. Assn., 1886), 8; General Conference of Seventh-day Adventists, *Seventh-day Adventist Year Book, 1892* (Battle Creek, MI: Review and Herald, 1892), 29; General Conference of Seventh-day Adventists, *Seventh-day Adventist Year Book, 1893* (Battle Creek, MI: General Conference Association of Seventh-day Adventists, 1893), 29; General Conference of Seventh-day Adventists, *Seventh-day Adventist Year Book, 1894* (Battle Creek, MI: General Conference Association of Seventh-day Adventists, 1894), 25, 86.

4. *The Seventh-day Encyclopedia*, s.v. "Trinidad and Tobago"; Enoch, *Glimpses of the Carribean*, 16. Hyatt, "Flowers," 735.

5. Tenney, "Death of Elder A. E. Flowers," 544; Sharp, "Mrs. E. W. Webster," 22. Enoch, *Glimpses of the Caribbean*, 18.

6. Adolph Johnson, "Webster," Obituaries, *Pacific Union Recorder* 34, no. 39 (April 24, 1935): 5; see also Adolph Johnson, "Webster," Obituaries, *North Pacific Union Gleaner* 30, no. 15 (April 9, 1935): 7; Enoch, *Glimpses of the Caribbean*, 18; see E. W. and L. A. Webster, "Trinidad, W. I.," *Review and Herald* 73, no. 27 (July 7, 1896): 424; E. W. Webster, "Trinidad, W. I.," *Review and Herald* 74, no. 26 (June 29, 1897): 409, which is signed only by Edwin, but it refers to Lucy's work and pays tribute to her as sharing in his labors.

7. E. W. Webster, "Experience With Yellow Fever," *Review and Herald* 75, no. 11 (March 15, 1898): 176; Enoch, *Glimpses of the Caribbean*, 22.

8. Sharp, "Mrs. E. W. Webster," 22. See also E. W. Webster, "West Indies," *Review and Herald* 77, no. 26 (June 26, 1900): 412.

9. A. J. Haysmer, "Babcock," Obituaries, *Review and Herald* 78, no. 36 (September 3, 1901): 580; cf. news note, *Review and Herald* 78, no 28 (July 9, 1901): 450.

10. Luther M. Crowther, quoted in "Our Work and Workers," *Signs of the Times* 26, no. 46 (November 14, 1900): 13.

11. Laura Crowley, quoted in "Trinidad, B. W. I.," *Review and Herald* 78, no. 40 (October 1, 1901): 641; Clarence Santee, "Crowther," Obituaries, *Review and Herald* 101, no. 1 (January 3, 1924): 22; Enoch, *Review and Herald* , 18.

12. Mrs. L. M. Crowther, "Crowther," Obituaries, *Review and Herald* 79, no. 1 (January 7, 1902): 14.

13. A. J. Haysmer, "Death of Brother A. M. Fischer," *Review and Herald* 79, no. 15 (April 15, 1902): 23.

14. "The Barbados Treatment Rooms," *Caribbean Watchman* 4, no. 1 (January 1906): 12; see also an advertisement in *Caribbean Watchman*, January 1906, iii; Mrs. E. E. Andross, "Early Days in Inter-America," *Review and Herald* 106, no. 40 (October 3, 1929): 19; General Conference of Seventh-day Adventists, *Seventh-day Adventist Year Book, 1907* (Washington, DC: Review and Herald®, 1907), 98, 99; George F. Enoch, "Eastern Caribbean Conference," *Review and Herald* 83, no. 10 (March 8, 1906): 18, 19.

15. O. E. Davis, "Obituary," *North Pacific Union Gleaner* 1, no. 49 (April 4, 1907): 4.

16. "At the Treatment Rooms" advertisement, *Caribbean Watchman* 5, no. 1 (January 1907), ii; the same advertisement is in *Caribbean Watchman* 5, no. 2 (February 1907). W. A. S[picer], "Two Vacant Places in the Mission Field Ranks," *Review and Herald* 84, no. 9 (February 28, 1907): 5.

17. S. A. Wellman to W. A. Spicer, quoted in Spicer, "Two Vacant Places," 5.

18. Resolution passed at the East Caribbean Conference and South Caribbean Conference Sessions, held jointly, December 1907, quoted in S. A. Wellman, "Conference Meetings in the West Indies," *Review and Herald* 85, no. 9 (February 27, 1908): 19. Davis, "Obituary," 4.

19. George F. Enoch, quoted in Spicer, "Two Vacant Places," 5.

20. S. A. Wellman, "Robert L. Price," *Caribbean Watchman* 6, no. 7 (July 1908): 12; cf. Spicer, "Two Vacant Places," 5; Mrs. Andross, "Early Days," 19.

21. Arthur E. Sutton, "Sutton," Necrology, *Inter-American Messenger* 41, no. 9 (September 1964): 12. See General Conference Executive Committee, minutes of meetings of Jan. 10, May 21, and July 17, 1918, GCA, Proceedings, vol. X, bk.. ii, p. 754, vol. XI, bk. i, pp. 37, 96. Sutton passport application, August 26, 1918, issued September 7, 1918, *U.S. Passport Applications, 1795–1925* (Lehi, UT: Ancestry.com, 2007), online database.

22. Haak passport application, February 5, 1914, *U.S. Passport Applications, 1795–1925* (Lehi, UT: Ancestry.com, 2007), online database; *UK, Incoming Passenger Lists, 1878–1960*

(Provo, UT: Ancestry.com, 2008), online database; *UK, Outward Passenger Lists, 1890–1960* (Provo, UT: Ancestry.com, 2012), online database; J. W. Westphal, "Elder B. C. Haak," *Review and Herald* 92, no. 4 (January 21, 1915): 14.

23. Westphal, "Elder B. C. Haak," 14; J. W. Westphal, "Argentine Annual Conference," *Review and Herald* , January 21, 1915, 14.

CHAPTER 5

"Whatever Sacrifice Is Necessary": The Far East and the South Pacific

Far away from Central and South America, on the other side of the Pacific Ocean, Adventist missionaries were beginning to penetrate East Asia and were suffering the consequences. As we will see in chapter 10, many missionaries survived the work in East Asia, living and providing many years of service there. Yet missionaries died in East Asia too.

W. C. and Elizabeth Grainger in Japan with an unnamed person.

In 1896, William C. Grainger, the president of Healdsburg College (now Pacific Union College), and his wife, Elizabeth, courageously accepted a call to go as missionaries to Japan at the ages of fifty-two and fifty-one respectively.[1] Being an educator, Grainger founded a school in Tokyo to teach the Bible; the school experienced some success, though reports were unclear as to whether students wanted to study the Bible or learn English. But Grainger's educational approach enjoyed sufficient success that four other missionaries were called to join the Graingers in 1898. In early October 1899, having been in Japan for just over three years, Grainger contracted an unknown illness. After suffering for more than three weeks, he died "of fever" on October 31 at the age of fifty-five. He is buried in Aoyama Cemetery in Tokyo.[2]

A church leader who had known the Graingers in California lamented the loss of "a true and faithful husband, . . . a loving and wise father, and . . . a genial, equable, helpful brother." A colleague who witnessed his passing wrote to friends at home: "He died the most triumphant death I ever heard of." This may be a way of rationalizing his suffering in the absence of miraculous healing, but it was probably also a way of saying that Grainger was of good courage in his last moments and that he wanted his colleagues to focus not on grief but on their work.[3]

Dr. Maude Amelia Thompson was a classmate of Dr. Harry W. Miller at the American Medical Missionary College. But Maude was a

Drs. Harry and Maude Miller at their wedding.

prodigy; at twenty-two years old, she was the youngest in her class. While the two doctors may have been attracted to each other, they may also have both been keen to go overseas as missionaries and knew the chances of being accepted for foreign mission service were greater if an applicant were married. Soon after they graduated on June 19, 1902, they were married on July 2, 1902. Though they both worked at the church's Chicago Sanitarium, they were "impressed with the need of the millions in China, [so] they volunteered to go and carry the gospel" there. In 1903, they were called to China and traveled across the Pacific Ocean to the interior of China. They arrived at their assigned station, Sin Tsai Hsien, in November 1903. According to colleagues, Maude "worked energetically in mastering the language and teaching the gospel as well as caring for the large number of sick children and women" that came "every day" for treatment.[4]

In the winter of 1903–1904, she developed sprue—a disease that was not well understood but which killed many Europeans in early twentieth-century Asia. (Maude's husband, Harry, later had to be sent home when suffering from the disease and almost died, though he was later able to return to China after World War I.) Maude's colleagues marveled, "During her illness her hope and courage found many expressions which we cherish to our comfort." They continued, paying tribute to their lost friend, "Although we do not understand the reason, we know God's ways are . . . above our ways. May the seed of a consecrated life laid down in the line of duty and self sacrifice be watered of God to bring forth a glorious harvest of souls from China ere the soon-coming of our King." Maude died on March 14, 1905, and her funeral was conducted by Dr. Arthur Selmon (whose career in China we will return to in chapter 10).[5]

Dr. Maude Thompson Miller in Chinese clothing.

Early in 1915, Elsie Morgan and Clarence Davis were married; they then accepted a call to go as missionaries to China. They sailed from Sydney on August 31, 1915, disembarked in Shanghai, and arrived in Nanjing on September 30. As one of their colleagues wrote, Clarence "little thought that they would be permitted to live together but six weeks in the mission field . . . for both were buoyant in faith." But Elsie "died in Nanking [Nanjing], China, November 12, 1915, after a brief illness of but ten hours." The same colleague noted, "Her sorrowing husband feels the hand of affliction heavy upon him," but Elsie died at peace. In her obituary, her dying words are reported as "Jesus knows all about it, and it is all right." She was only twenty-two years old and died before she had seen barely anything of the world, much less her chosen mission field.[6]

Yet her passing was used as an occasion for urging greater missionary effort. Elsie and Clarence were some of the first Australian Seventh-day Adventist missionaries to China, and Elsie was the first to die there. Her obituary comments that "surely it will be a day of affliction to our people in Australia, for of the workers furnished to this field, Sister Davis is the first to fall at her post; but may not her death be a call to the young men and women of the Australasian Union to consecrate their lives for service in the needy Orient?"[7]

But Elsie Davis was not the last to lose her life swiftly in China. On August 14, 1930, Dr. Elmer F. Coulston, a graduate of the College of Medical Evangelists in Loma Linda, California, married Leatha Wenke, a nursing graduate of Emmanuel Missionary College and Battle Creek Sanitarium. Both were twenty-four years old. They were another missionary couple for whom their voyage to the mission field was their honeymoon: as barely two weeks after their wedding, they sailed for China from San Francisco. Nearly four weeks later, on September 25, Elmer and Leatha arrived in Shanghai and went on to Beijing to begin studying Chinese. After a year of learning the language, they traveled northwest to what the China Division president called "the distant frontier city of Kalgan." Known today as Zhangjiakou, in the Hebei Province, Kalgan was the location of the North China Sanitarium, which was still under construction. Dr. Coulston was its first medical superintendent. He threw himself unreservedly into the medical-ministry work that he had been "very interested" in for years, for he had "followed with intense interest the development of . . . [the church's] medical work in the foreign fields." Elmer and Leatha were, he wrote to a General Conference official, "anxious to begin our work."[8]

On November 30, 1931, a son, Chris, was born in Kalgan. Sadly, little Chris was buried there too. He died on October 4, 1932; he was

Elmer F. Coulston.

only ten months old.[9] Tragically, less than two years later, Elmer contracted "a virulent type of diphtheria." Although taken for treatment 120 miles south to Beijing, he died on May 26, 1934, having suffered for one week. His body was taken back to Kalgan and buried in the same grave as his son.[10] He had served as a missionary for three years and eight months and was only twenty-eight years old.

Elmer was young, charismatic, and magnetic; remarkably fluent in Chinese; and generally judged to possess "brilliant talents." His death was regarded as a "terrible loss" by non-Adventist expatriates in northern China and church workers both inside and outside China. He was "deeply mourned" by the local community in Kalgan, who joined missionaries and local believers in the funeral service. Yet his "sudden illness and death" did not come entirely as a surprise.[11]

In his three years at Kalgan, he was often ill, regularly "battling with pleurisy and fever." The problem was that he prioritized his patients ahead of himself. He commonly worked closely with highly contagious patients, showing Christian love as well as giving medical care. When ill, he did not take sufficient

Elmer and Chris Coulston's tomb in China.

care of himself. A year before his death, he required a major surgery, "which of necessity required that he remain in bed for many days." But "a few days after his operation an acute case whose life depended on surgery was brought to the hospital." Coulston had "the sick man . . . placed on a cot by his bed, and he, while lying down, reached over and successfully operated on this patient, saving his life."[12]

Leatha Coulston at Elmer's funeral, being comforted by other missionary wives.

Even in Elmer's final illness, after falling ill on a Friday, on "Sunday he responded to an emergency call, labouring over a dying person . . . for three hours until exhausted." Having "learned to love" the Chinese people, Elmer and Leatha let nothing stand in the way of modeling Christ's healing ministry to them. In hindsight, it is no surprise that the physician was susceptible to a fatal infection and lacked the strength to fight it off.[13]

Elmer F. Coulston had been mentored by Dr. Harry Miller, who was Maude Miller's widower, president of the China Division, and a surgeon himself. Miller identified the underlying cause of his protégé's death as overwork, commenting, "His one fault was working beyond his strength." But Elmer had told Miller shortly after arriving in China, " 'Whatever sacrifice is necessary, I shall willingly make for my Master. Truly, I shall be at the "front line trenches." ' "[14]

Before modern medicines, diseases were particular risks in the islands of the tropical zone banding the world. In 1894, Julia Caldwell and her husband, Dr. Joseph E. Caldwell, sailed on the mission ship *Pitcairn* during its third mission voyage; they landed at Rarotonga in the Cook Islands on October 9, 1894. Both had considerable intellectual gifts. Joseph was twice a doctor, with both an MD and a PhD, and was also an ordained minister. He praised Julia's "sound judgment," and using her intellectual gifts, she set up a mission school in Rarotonga. For six years she taught there while Joseph, who a colleague described as "a kind, sympathetic worker," provided medical care to the islanders.[15]

By 1900, Julia was suffering badly from what was reported at the time as a "fever," though it is difficult to know just which disease it was. In February 1901, the Caldwells sailed for New Zealand, where they hoped to find a cure for Julia. But as Joseph grimly noted, it was too late: "she being broken in health." After several apparent recoveries and relapses, she went into a monthlong final illness. "Yes, thank the Lord," were her final words, spoken on March 1, 1902. As one Adventist scholar writes, she was worn out by "the effects of heat and deprivation during her . . . sacrificial service on Rarotonga."[16]

In 1900, the Caldwells had been joined in the Cook Islands by Albert H. Piper and his wife, Hester, known as Hettie. They were the first in a long line of Australasian missionaries to go to the islands of the South Pacific. Albert and Hettie were only twenty-five years of age when they began their service of nearly seven years in Rarotonga. They had a brief furlough in New Zealand in 1904, when Albert was ordained, and could have remained in their homeland. Yet, in spite of having seen what Julia Caldwell had suffered, Albert and Hettie returned to Rarotonga. Hettie contracted tuberculosis, and they returned to New Zealand and then went on to Australia in 1907. Her health never recovered. As it worsened, her two sons were sent to live with an aunt. Laurence, the younger boy, wrote to his mother:

Dear Mama,

I will try to be such a good boy that if I do not see you again on this earth I will meet you when Jesus comes to take us home.

But Hettie "was not afraid of death. Worn out by the cruel disease, she longed to rest. Her last words were, 'I am so happy.' " Hettie Piper died on June 1, 1912, at the age of thirty-seven.[17]

In June 1902—the summer following Julia Caldwell's death—two young physicians, Alfred Martin Vollmer and Maude Otis, graduated from the American Medical Missionary College. The following spring Alfred accepted a call from the General Conference to serve at the sanitarium in Samoa. Perhaps the call depended on Vollmer being married, as was somewhat typical in that era, or maybe he and Maude meant to marry; in any case, the two former classmates wed on July 14, 1903. He was twenty-seven, and she twenty-four. They sailed in October and arrived in Apia on November 12, 1903. And in Apia, their only child—a daughter named Dorothea—was born on Septmber 26, 1904.[18]

Alfred Martin Vollmer and Maude Otis at their graduation.

Alfred contracted tuberculosis. "He loved the work in that field, and when he was compelled to leave on account of his health, it was with the deepest regret." In October 1905, having served not quite two years after arriving in Apia, Alfred was sent back to the States for treatment, and his family went with him. He was "very sick" on the voyage home, but as his obituary observes: "The Lord was merciful, and spared his life to reach his home." Alfred did not long survive his return and "suffered a great deal the last few weeks of his life." Alfred Vollmer died on February 15, 1906—eight days short of his thirtieth birthday.[19]

After twenty-three months of mission service, Maude was a widow at the age of twenty-seven, and Dorothea was fatherless at twenty months.

The Vollmers had been joined in Samoa by Sarah Mareta Young; she was a native of Pitcairn Island who had graduated as a nurse from Sydney Sanitarium in 1903 and went to Samoa in May 1904. Five months after Vollmer's death, in mid-July 1906, Sarah died of pneumonia. "She was loved by all who knew her," according to an Adventist physician who worked with her. Her last letter to friends on July 1, 1906, urged, "May many more be found who are ready to say, 'Here am I, send me.' " Sarah perished just two years and two months after she joined the Samoa Sanitarium.[20]

The case of Sarah Mareta Young reminds us that Westerners were not the only ones who went as missionaries and they were not the only ones who died. Another such missionary was Bennie (or Peni) Tavodi, who was a Fijian convert. He went to serve in Papua (now Papua New Guinea) in June 1908. Tavodi served there for more than a decade, but in October 1918, he died at Bisiatabu Mission, Papua, from a snakebite. His last moments were spent encouraging those around him "to yield themselves to the Lord." The mission superintendent, A. N. Lawson, wrote movingly to a friend: "I don't think it is necessary for me to describe to you my feelings; how I was hoping and praying that the Lord would spare his life a little longer, and just how I felt when I . . . knew that all was over." Lawson continued, "I held a memorial service . . . Sabbath morning" for those living around the mission station, "and though being heartbroken myself" was able to "speak . . . comforting promises."[21]

The next several years would see more tragic early deaths in the islands of the Pacific. In 1915, Hubert Leonard Tolhurst and Pearl Philps, two young graduates of the Australasian Missionary College, married: they had fallen in love as students and were married in January. Hubert was twenty-four years old, and Pearl was twenty-three. Like so many missionaries of this era, within weeks of their wedding, they set out for the mission field. In their case, they sailed for the Tongan archipelago in February 1915 "to take charge of [a] mission station" on "an isolated island group known as Ha'apai."[22]

Looking back, those were "busy and happy years" for the couple, but Hubert and Pearl started to suffer sustained illnesses. By late 1918, the church leaders in Australia received "tidings . . . that Sister Tolhurst's health was failing," and they sent messages for the couple "to return to Sydney." But it was too late. The global influenza epidemic of 1918 had reached Tonga, and both Hubert and Pearl "in their weakened physical condition readily took the disease." Despite this, as an obituary describes, they worked "long hours ministering to the sick and stricken people, and then [they] succumbed to the plague themselves." Hubert recovered relatively quickly, but after nearly "four years of wearing toil in the mission field," Pearl, who suffered both influenza and pneumonia, was drained. She "gradually grew weaker. After a four-months' struggle for life she fell asleep in his [Hubert's] arms," dying on March 14, 1919, four days after her twenty-eighth birthday.[23]

Hubert's anguish could not be articulated easily, given the rhetorical constraints of the era. But as with some other grieving spouses, it suddenly becomes evident in little points of detail. It is there, for example, when he writes: "She suffered much, knowing no bodily comfort for many weeks. And often the cough was most distressing." His pain is even more apparent in a comment in her obituary: "The writer had to conduct the service."[24]

Pearl had been in the islands for four years. Her parents greeted the news of her death with a sense of willing sacrifice: "It came as a great shock. . . . But God's will be done. Our dear girl has fallen at her post and we thank the dear Lord that He has seen fit to use her for a time in His cause. . . . We feel deeply burdened about the work in Haapai and will gladly release another of our girls if it will help, till another worker is appointed." Remarkably, this offer was to be taken up.[25]

Back in Australia, Hubert became better acquainted with Elsmer, one of Pearl's sisters who was a teacher. They married on March 15, 1921, and accepted a call to Tonga. Hubert and Elsmer served in Tonga, New Zealand, and other islands of the South Pacific for the next twenty years.[26]

Pearl Philps and her sisters in 1907, eight years before she married Hubert.

Not long before Hubert and Pearl married, another pair of students from the Australasian Missionary College were wed. In late 1914, having just graduated, Norman Wiles volunteered to serve in the New Hebrides (today's nation of Vanuatu). But he was single, and the Australasian Union committee felt that a missionary ought to be married. During his college years, Norman had been friends with Alma Butz, herself the daughter of American missionaries to Pitcairn Island, Tonga, New Zealand, and Australia.

It was suggested that Norman marry Alma, and then they could be sent. She later recalled her anger, writing, "I would not submit. . . . I would not be bought or sold by committee action." But after her mother counseled with her, she cooled down and agreed to meet Norman. According to Alma, "We talked over the advisability and the future possibilities at some length. Norman never proposed in the usual way. We simply felt that if this was the action of the committee, the Lord was leading and that settled the matter."[27]

This is how some things were done a century ago! Love of God and His mission were put above romantic love; instead, it was assumed that where there was one, the other would follow (and so it usually proved). Norman and Alma married on December 24, 1914.[28]

In early 1915, the newlyweds studied at Sydney Sanitarium, taking a course in tropical medicine. Later that year, they sailed for the New Hebrides, where they initially worked as part of a larger group of missionaries based in Atchin. It was in Atchin that Alma's father, Edwin Butz, and fellow American missionaries C. H. Parker and Harold Carr had bought land and established a mission station in 1912. By February 1916, Norman and Alma began preparing to establish a new mission station on the much larger island of Malekula. In early April, when Norman was twenty-three and Alma twenty-one, they took up residence there—the sole missionaries on the island. The tribes who lived on the

Norman and Alma Wiles around 1915.

island included "warlike cannibals," and the murders of missionaries and European traders were not uncommon. In mid-1916, a local chief "vowed to eat nothing until he had feasted on the flesh of a white man," and "Norman was the only white man available."[29]

For the next two years, he and Alma won the local people over, learning their languages and making friends.

By October 1917, the church leaders in Australia recognized that Norman and Alma had "been working to the point of breaking down

Norman and Alva Wiles made friends with the islanders. This is evident from their relaxed stance.

their health," so they "felt obliged to send them home to build up again." In November, Norman was suffering badly from "repeated attacks of malaria," and, according to another missionary, was "very pale and thin." In 1918, Norman filled responsibilities back in his homeland. In January 1920, however, to the Wileses' delight, they "returned to Malekula." By April, they were receiving requests for Adventist teachers from tribes on the island who had never before contacted them. But because these missionaries had won the trust of other tribes, they turned to them to settle disputes and broker peace between tribes with longstanding enmities.[30]

But then on Sabbath, May 1, 1920, Norman succumbed to black-water fever. Alma's diary notes that in the "afternoon we questioned what percent of the disease was fatal." By the third, Norman was "vomiting all the time, and suffering from chills." By the fifth, Alma confided her anxiety to her diary in terms that still have the power to move readers: "Hard as it all was, my Father strengthened my faith, so that I never once doubted, nor was my confidence in Him shaken. . . . Again and again I pled that if it could be to His honor and glory, my darling might be spared me, but He gave me strength to add, 'Thy will be done.' "[31]

Around ten in the evening on May 5, 1920, Norman Wiles died after five days of terrible suffering. Alma dressed her husband's body in a new shirt and then covered his corpse in a shroud. Friendly tribesmen helped her to dig a grave and bury Norman in it. She wrote that her heart "was too full for words," so she "just stood silently." With some difficulty, she eventually made it to Atchin and the island's Adventist mission station.[32]

One of the workers on Atchin, A. G. Stewart, reflected on the news of Norman's passing, seeking consolation and meaning as did many other grieving colleagues: "Surely there are others who will come and pick up the fallen standard. These are no doubt some of the trials we are permitted to bear in helping to gather lost ones into the fold. If the sacrifice is not in vain we shall feel more than repaid." Norman Wiles died a few months before Eva Clements, and the church leaders in Australia, including Hubert Tolhurst, expressed their hope that the sacrifices of Elsie Davis, Pearl Tolhurst, Norman Wiles, and Eva Clements "constituted a strong appeal to our dear young people in Australia to volunteer for service."[33]

These attempts to find consolation or inspiration were sincere but should not distract us from a harsh reality. Norman was only twenty-seven years old when he died; Alma was twenty-five when she was widowed. Altogether, they had served about four years as missionaries.

But there is an extraordinary coda to this story: just as Hubert Tolhurst returned to Pacific Island mission fields, so, too, did Alma

Wiles. After Norman's death, she went back to Australia and was admitted to the Sydney Sanitarium. But time healed some wounds. She later went to the United States to study and in 1934 went as a missionary to Papua New Guinea, which is not far from Vanuatu.

Alma Wiles in later years.

She served there for seven years until she was evacuated following the outbreak of war with Japan. She spent the next seventeen years in Australia; in November 1959, at the age of sixty-five, she volunteered to serve in Nigeria and spent three years as the head of the midwife training program at Ile-Ife Hospital.[34] A passion for mission ran deep in Alma's soul—and in those of many of her contemporaries.

1. News note, *Review and Herald* 76, no. 49 (December 5, 1899): 796.

2. U[riah] S[mith], "A Sad Harvest," *Review and Herald* 77, no. 3 (January 16, 1900): 48; "Fallen at His Post," *Signs of the Times* 25, no. 51 (December 20, 1899): 16.

3. "Fallen at His Post," 16; news note, *Review and Herald*, December 5, 1899, 796.

4. Carrie Errichson and Charlotte Simpson, "Miller," Obituaries, *West Michigan Herald* 3, no. 18 (May 10, 1905): 3.

5. Errichson and Simpson, "Miller," 3.

6. W. W. Fletcher, "Workers Sail for China," *Australasian Record* 19, no. 36 (September 6, 1915): 8; James E. Shultz, "Another Worker Fallen," *Australasian Record* 20, no. 4 (January 31, 1916): 2, 3.

7. Shultz, "Another Worker Fallen," 3.

8. Elmer F. Coulston to Foreign Mission Board, September 27, 1929; Elmer F. Coulston to M. E. Kern, August 26, 1930, GCA, Record Group 21, missionary appointee file no. 45516; H. W. Miller to P. T. Magan, June 4, 1934, copy enclosed with H. W. Miller to L. C. Coulston, June 4, 1934, Elmer F. Coulston Collection, Department of Archives and Special Collections, Loma Linda University; H. W. Miller, "Dr. E. F. Coulston," Asleep in Jesus, *Review and Herald* 111, no. 33 (August 16, 1934): 21, see also Obituary, *China Division Reporter* 4, no. 7 (July 1934): 22; Harry W. Miller, "Memoirs to the Late Doctor Coulston: Address at the Funeral in Peiping and Kalgan, May 29, 1934," *China Division Reporter*, July 1934, 22, 23. See also Elmer F. Coulston, "The North China Sanitarium and Hospital," *China Division Reporter*, July 1934, 15, 16.

9. George J. Appel, [Chris Coulston], Obituary, *China Division Reporter* 2, nos. 9, 10 (September/October 1932): 8; Chris Coulston, death notification, November 5, 1932, "Report of the Death of an American Citizen," US State Department Decimal Files, 1910–1963, United States National Archives, College Park, MD. Record Group 59, Box 1813, 1930–1939 China Br-Fu.

10. Miller to Magan, June 4, 1934; Miller, "Dr. E. F. Coulston," 21; Miller, "Memoirs to the Late Doctor," 22.

11. D. H. Gray, "Died at His Post," *Australasian Record* 38, no. 42 (October 15, 1934): 2, 3; "From Pastor Geo. J. Appel," *China Division Reporter* 4, no. 7 (July 1934): 3; H. W. Miller, quoted in Gray, "Died at His Post," 3. See the collection of report clippings on Coulston's death in Chinese and

American newspapers (not church papers) in Loma Linda University's Elmer F. Coulston Collection.

12. Miller, quoted in Gray, "Died at His Post," 2. See also Coulston, "North China Sanitarium," 15, 16.

13. Miller, quoted in Gray, "Died at His Post," 3; Miller, "Dr. E. F. Coulston," 21; Obituary, *China Division Reporter*, July 1934, 22.

14. Miller, "Memoirs to the Late Doctor," 23; Miller, quoted in Gray, "Died at His Post," 2, emphasis added.

15. J. E. Caldwell, "Another Worker Fallen," Obituaries, *Review and Herald* 79, no. 15 (April 15, 1902): 23; R. W. Parmele, "Dr. J. E. Caldwell," Obituaries, *Review and Herald* 100, no. 47 (November 22, 1923): 22.

16. Caldwell, "Another Worker Fallen," 23; Marye Trim, *Courage in the Lord: The Story of Albert Henry Piper* (Sydney, Australia: Education Department, South Pacific Division of Seventh-day Adventists, 2004), 17.

17. Trim, *Courage*, 15–22 (Lawrence's letter is printed on page 21); J. E. Fulton, "Piper," Obituary, *Australasian Record* 16, no. 25 (June 17, 1912): 7.

18. "Commencement Exercises of the American Medical Missionary College," *Review and Herald* 79, no. 30 (July 29, 1902): 9; "The A. M. M. C. Representatives," *Review and Herald*, July 29, 1902, 12; "Vollmer," Obituaries, *Review and Herald* 83, no. 13 (March 29, 1906): 23; "Vollmer," In Remembrance, *Review and Herald* 143, no. 37 (August 4, 1966): 25; minutes of meeting of May 1, 1903, GCA, Proceedings, vol. VI, p. 28; *Cook County, Illinois, Marriages Index, 1871–1920* (Provo, UT: Ancestry.com, 2011), online database; Milton Hook, *Loto aso fitu: Early Adventism in Samoa*, Seventh-day Adventist Heritage 22 (Wahroonga, NSW, Australia: Department of Education, South Pacific Division of Seventh-day Adventists, n.d.), 8; "Field Notes," *Review and Herald* 80, no. 52 (December 31, 1903): 20.

19. "Vollmer," *Review and Herald*, March 29, 1906, 23. Hook, *Loto aso fitu*, 9.

20. Hook, *Loto aso fitu*, 9; F. E. Braucht, quoted in *Review and Herald* 83, no. 39 (September 27, 1906): 24; Sarah Mareta Young, quoted in *Union Conference Record* [*Australasian Record*] 10, no. 17 (August 20, 1906): 12.

21. W. A. S[picer], "To the Fields in 1908," *Review and Herald* 86, no. 1 (January 7, 1909): 6. A. N. Lawson, quoted in "The Death of Bennie Tavodi," *Australasian Record* 22, no. 25 (December 9, 1918): 6. "Bennie" seems to have been the Anglicization of the Fijian *Peni*, which is the version of Tavodi's name that Robert Dixon used in his chapter, "The Pacific Islands," in *Seventh-day Adventists in the South Pacific, 1885–1985*, ed. Noel Clapham (Warburton, Australia: Signs Pub., 1985), 202, 208, 211.

22. H. L. Tolhurst, "Tolhurst," Obituaries, *Australasian Record* 23, no. 12 (May 26, 1919): 7; "Life-Sketch of Pastor H. L. Tolhurst," *Australasian Record* 86, no. 50 (December 14, 1981): 13.

23. "Life-Sketch of Pastor H. L. Tolhurst," 13; C. H. Prettyman, "The Death of Sister Pearl Tolhurst," *Australasian Record*, May 26, 1919, 8; Tolhurst, "Tolhurst," 7.

24. Tolhurst, "Tolhurst," 7; information also from Athal Tolhurst, Hubert Tolhurst's son.

25. Prettyman, "Death of Sister Pearl Tolhurst," 8.

26. For H. L. Tolhurst's marriage to Elsmer, see "Life-Sketch of Pastor H. L. Tolhurst," 13.

27. Roy Brandstater, *Man-Eaters of Malekula* (Nampa, ID: Pacific Press®, 2017), 46.

28. Brandstater, *Man-Eaters*, 132.

29. H. M. Blunden, "In the New Hebrides: No. 4—In the Perils of the Heathen," *Australasian Record* 26, no. 1 (January 9, 1922): 2, 3; Brandstater, *Man-Eaters*, 46, 54, 55, and see also 35, 46–49, 51, 53, 132; C. H. Parker, "Atchin, New Hebrides," *Australasian Record* 19, no. 25 (June 21, 1915): 4.

30. G. F. Jones, "The Melanesian Mission," in "Reports of Tenth Session of the Australasian Union Conference," special issue no. 1, *Australasian Record* 22, no. 22 (October 21, 1918): 54; Letter from Sister Jones, quoted in *Australasian Record* 21, no. 39 (December 17, 1917): 8; Brandstater, *Man-Eaters*, 58, 60.

31. Brandstater, *Man-Eaters*, 61, 62, 65, 66.

32. Brandstater, *Man-Eaters*, 62, 66–68, 70–74; see also A. G. Stewart, "Wiles," Obituary, *Australasian Record* 24, no. 16 (August 9, 1920): 6.

33. Letter from A. G. Stewart, quoted in *Australasian Record*, August 9, 1920, 8. H. L. Tolhurst, "Another Call," *Australasian Record* 24, no. 25 (December 13, 1920): 8; cf. W. G. Turner, "Union Conference Secretary's Report," *Australasian Record* 25, no. 18 (September 5, 1921): 2.

34. Brandstater, *Man-Eaters*, 133, 134.

CHAPTER 6

"Exposed to Many Hardships": The Middle East and the Mediterranean

E ven though the tropics were particularly dangerous for early missionaries, lethal diseases were present all around the world, including in zones better known for deserts than jungles. For example, in January 1904, J. G. Teschner, a German nurse of whom almost nothing is known, arrived in Jerusalem, where he was to work in the church's clinic there. On July 26, 1904, he died of an unknown illness. As the *Review and Herald* reported, he "had but landed in Syria . . . when he was called to lay down the armor." He did not serve even a year before he died: he was probably the first German Seventh-day Adventist missionary to do so in the field. The General Conference secretary, William Spicer, drew the attention of the *Review*'s American readers to Teschner's sacrifice: "Thus our brethren in Europe show that . . . they, too, are ready to join us in giving not only means for the missionary advance" but also in paying "the price that soldiers must ever be ready to pay for victory."[1]

In 1902, William H. Wakeham, his wife, Emma, and their children were called to Egypt, where Wakeham was to be the superintendent

of the Oriental Union Mission. During the nearly four years they served in the Middle East. William was conscientious and industrious, journeying widely across the region to provide leadership and training to local church workers and other missionaries; the photograph on the next page shows him with one such group. Although William was the one who was traveling and experiencing the associated dangers from the elements

W. H. Wakeham.

and from hostile agents (human, viral, or bacterial), Emma and their children were exposed to illnesses while also experiencing privation and periodic uncertainty about their husband and father's fate—or even his whereabouts. One of William's colleagues later wrote, "The family were exposed to many hardships, and suffered from smallpox and other diseases" during their years in Egypt.[2]

W. H. Wakeham with a group of Armenian church workers at a Bible training institute in late 1905.

However, "Sister Wakeham, being a trained nurse, was able by the Lord's help to bring her children through this trying ordeal; but with the extreme heat of Egypt, in addition to what she had otherwise endured, her health broke." On May 4, 1906, the family boarded a ship for the British port of Southampton, "hoping that the sea voyage would greatly relieve Sister Wakeham." By this point, her husband wrote, she was suffering "a rapid breaking down of all the vital powers." They hoped that the medical treatments available in the West would effect a cure.[3]

But Emma never made it to England. She died while the ship was still at sea. She was buried at sea on May 13, 1906. William emotionally recorded the death of his "dear wife, Emma . . . in her forty-sixth year." In his tribute to her, his sense of loss pierces the veil of stoicism his public report attempted to draw over his grief:

> "She has always been a loving wife, a devoted mother, an unselfish and untiring worker for suffering humanity. Four children, two boys and two girls, feel keenly this great loss. . . . With hearts sad and sore, yet buoyed up by the blessed hope, we committed her body to [the] old ocean's arms, confident that, though no monument marks her resting-place, she will not be overlooked when the Life-giver calls the sleeping saints. . . . We do not know the meaning of this bereavement. Our loss! Egypt's loss."[4]

That same year Dr. Arthur W. George, a medical missionary, became the director of the Turkish Mission, having arrived in Constantinople (today's Istanbul) in November 1903. He worked hard to learn French, the language of Ottoman medical examinations, and opened treatment rooms in Constantinople. However, he contracted what at first seemed like influenza but was eventually confirmed as tuberculosis. Dr. George was "a faithful worker in both medical and evangelistic effort," wrote a church leader. "He clung to his work too long for the good of his health," noted a fellow missionary to the Middle East. In the end, a successor was called from America—Claude D. AcMoody—but Dr. George was so ill that he could not wait for a transfer of duties. On November 23, 1906, just ten days before AcMoody arrived, Dr. George and his wife, Johanna (who he had married only seventeen months before), left the Turkish capital by train for Switzerland. He was taken to the Adventist sanitarium in Gland, Switzerland (today's Clinique La Lignière), and then to Friedensau Sanitarium in Germany. But he had left it too late to seek treatment.[5]

After three years' service as a missionary, Arthur W. George passed away, at the age of thirty-four, on February 13, 1907.

The reaction of his brother, who was another physician, on learning of Arthur's death was similar to that of many other bereaved family members of Adventist missionaries: "I hope that the work in Turkey will be in no way hindered, but that his death may only stimulate others to take up the work and do more. . . . If so, we can feel that our sacrifice in giving him up will be repaid." There was consolation in the thought that individual sacrifice might lead to salvation for many.[6]

Dr. George's successor, the twenty-four-year-old Claude AcMoody, arrived in Constantinople on December 3, 1906. AcMoody had graduated from Battle Creek College in 1902 and began pastoring in Wisconsin. In July 1904, he married, but rather than settling down, he and his wife, Henrietta, decided within their first year of marriage that they wanted to serve as missionaries. In 1905, Claude joined the second class to study at the recently opened Washington Training College. (In 1907, it would be renamed Washington Foreign Mission Seminary, but in 1905, it was already a General Conference institution focused on training those who were willing to serve overseas for the particular challenges they would face.) So committed were Claude and Henrietta that he enrolled in the college—even though Henrietta was expecting their first child, was having a difficult pregnancy, and could not travel. In the autumn of 1905, Claude moved to Washington, DC, without Henrietta but accompanied by his brother Clayton. Claude and his mother, Florence, went to Wisconsin for Henrietta's confinement, no doubt expecting that she would return with them to Washington. Sadly, Henrietta died on September 24, 1905—just four months after giving birth to a daughter, and the infant died soon after her.[7]

Claude returned and completed a yearlong course. While studying, he was considered for mission service in French-speaking Canada; yet within weeks of completing his studies, he was called to the Ottoman Empire—presumably, he already knew French (unlike Arthur George). Claude submitted his application for his first United States passport on October 30, 1906. By an odd coincidence, not long before, the Young People's Society of Takoma Park, of which Claude and Clayton were members, had G. F. Enoch, missionary to Trinidad, as its guest speaker on Sabbath—this was the same George Enoch whose brother Charles died just four months later. Claude spent time with his parents and sailed for Europe on November 8, 1906. He traveled across Germany and Romania by train and then by ship to Constantinople, arriving on December 3.[8]

We know that Claude was a temperance advocate and was

enthusiastic about both public evangelism and personal witnessing. His brother Clayton, with whom he was close, was a talented singer and an avid reader, and perhaps the two had these qualities in common. Claude certainly seems to have been characterized by empathy. This is evident in the only known photograph of him taken during his time working with the Turks. Its caption on the back reads simply: "A group of believers in Asia Minor, c.1907. Elder Claude AcMoody standing in rear." Unlike some Western missionaries, he did not position himself front and center in a place of honor. He stands modestly in the last row of the group, which consists of people of all ages. Many are smiling, at ease with this foreigner—so much so that the men are happy for their wives and children to mix with him. This speaks eloquently about Claude AcMoody's character. His personal experiences of tragedy may well have made him a more effective missionary.

Claude D. AcMoody with Turkish believers.

AcMoody did not remain cloistered in Constantinople. Within four days of landing at the imperial capital, he had begun his first itinerary, traveling first by ship and then by road. He went out and worked among the ordinary people of the Ottoman Empire rather than targeting expatriate Westerners.[9]

Working in the hinterlands, however, entailed risk. AcMoody had not been in Asia Minor long when, like Dr. George before him, he contracted pulmonary tuberculosis. Fifteen months after his arrival, the General Conference executive committee had to consider a replacement for him, and it voted to "advise Brother AcMoody to be careful to his health." But he had a vast territory to cover. The church leaders reduced it in an attempt to make it manageable; however, Claude was either unwilling or felt unable to take their advice. Furthermore, as a missionary leader later recalled, "he was determined to remain at his post of duty as long as possible." This exacerbated his condition. He reported to the church leaders in Washington, DC, that he was so "afflicted" by poor health that he "found it necessary . . . to make immediate plans to come to America," and he did, in fact, return to America. He left Constantinople on January 10, 1909, and arrived in New York City on February 5, 1909.[10]

A colleague wrote that Claude "hoped, after a brief sojourn in his native land, sufficiently to recover his health to resume his missionary labors in his chosen field; but in this he was disappointed. The disease made steady progress till the end came." C. D. AcMoody died in Long Beach, California, on July 23, 1911, after a long-drawn-out illness, not yet thirty years old. His service in the mission field, which effectively killed him, lasted only twenty-five months.[11]

Arthur George and Claude AcMoody had serious illnesses that were exacerbated by their tendency to overwork. Around the same time, the same was true of Thomas French, though he escaped with his life (chapter 3). And years later, overwork contributed to the death of Elmer Coulston (chapter 5). The inclination to overwork was typical of many other missionaries.

This tendency toward overwork meant that missionaries were not safe from early deaths—even in Western countries.

Walter G. Bond, a native of California and a graduate of Healdsburg College (Pacific Union College), married Leola Gerow in November 1902, less than a month after her nineteenth birthday. Like others before them, they had already accepted a call that was conditional on their marriage; almost immediately after the wedding, they sailed for Europe as missionaries, arriving in England in December. After studying for several months at the Adventist training school in London (today's Newbold College), where Walter celebrated his twenty-fourth birthday, the young missionary couple went on to Spain, reaching the Mediterranean city of Barcelona on June 22, 1903.[12]

Walter and Leola had served in Spain for eleven years when he joined a Spanish worker in the small southeastern city of Baeza in order to conduct evangelistic meetings. In his last report, Bond called Baeza "probably the most difficult place that we have thus far entered." Evangelizing in such circumstances took a toll. Two or three weeks into the campaign, Walter collapsed with acute peritonitis. His brother Frank, who was also a minister, was able to join him and later starkly recorded: "His suffering was intense." On November 12, 1914, Walter passed away at the age of thirty-five. He left "sorrowing" his widow and three young children—Paul, Elsa, and Frances, respectively ten, seven, and three years old.[13]

Walter's colleague Elmer Andross published a notice of Walter's passing in the *Pacific Union Recorder*, which combines, as is so often present in the life sketches of deceased missionaries, sadness and a call to service: "It is with joy that we look forward, through the clouds and through our tears, to the glorious morning of deliverance that is even now breaking over this dark world. Let us take up the standard that falls from the hands of the worn and weary soldier who is cut down at his post, and carry it on to a glorious and speedy triumph."[14]

Walter Bond in the last year of his life.

Overwork could take a toll anywhere. It was particularly prevalent in the mission fields of Africa and Asia, where there were far fewer Seventh-day Adventists, and thus far greater burdens fell on those who led the missionary efforts. Overwork was undoubtedly a contributing factor in the death of Dores A. Robinson in India in 1899. Robinson was the first superintendent of the India Mission, and his death was the first of many among the church's missionaries to what, in 1919, would become the Southern Asia Division. It is to India, Burma, Sri Lanka, Pakistan, and Bangladesh—all British colonies in the early twentieth century—that we now turn.

1. W. A. S[picer], "To Mission Fields in 1904," *Review and Herald* 82, no. 1 (January 5, 1905): 5; General Conference of Seventh-day Adventists, *Year Book of the Seventh-day Adventist Denomination, 1905* (Washington, DC: Review and Herald*, 1905), 130; W. A. S[picer], "The Price of Victory," *Review and Herald* 83, no. 3 (January 18, 1906): 5.

2. E. E. Andross, untitled article, In Memoriam, *Missionary Worker* 10, no. 11 (May 23, 1906): 87.

3. Ibid.; W. H. Wakeham, "Wakeham," Obituaries, *Review and Herald* 83, no. 25 (June 21, 1906): 23.

4. Wakeham, "Wakeham," 23.

5. W. A. S[picer], "Two Vacant Places in the Mission Field Ranks," *Review and Herald* 84, no. 9 (February 28, 1907): 5; C. D. AcMoody, "The Turkish Mission," *General Conference Bulletin* 6, no. 11 (May 26, 1909): 167. See L. R. Conradi, "A Faithful Laborer Fallen," *Review and Herald* 84, no. 12 (March 21, 1907): 24; L. R. Conradi, "George," Obituaries, *Review and Herald* 84, no. 15 (April 11, 1907): 23.

6. W. A. George, quoted in Spicer, "Two Vacant Places," 5.

7. See E. E. Andross, "Elder C. D. AcMoody," Obituaries, *Review and Herald* 88, no. 48 (November 24, 1911): 23. "Takma Park," *Washington Post*, December 10, 1905, 6; William Covert, "AcMoody," Obituaries, *Review and Herald* 82, no. 42 (October 19, 1905): 23.

8. AcMoody passport application, October 30, 1906, *U.S. Passport Applications, 1795–1925* (Lehi, UT: Ancestry.com, 2007), online database; news note, *Review and Herald* 83, no. 41 (October 11, 1906): 24; "Takoma Park," *Washington Post*, November 4, 1906, 6; news note, *Review and Herald* 83, no. 46 (November 15, 1906): 24; C. D. AcMoody, "From Hamburg to Turkey," *Review and Herald* 84, no. 10 (March 7, 1907): 14; AcMoody, "Turkish Mission," 168.

9. AcMoody, "From Hamburg to Turkey," 14; AcMoody, "Turkish Mission," 168.

10. General Conference Executive Committee, meeting of March 14, 1908, *Proceedings*, vol. VII, pp. 420–21, quotation at p. 420; Andross, "Elder C. D. AcMoody," 23; AcMoody, "Turkish Mission," 168, 169; *New York, Passenger and Crew Lists (Including Castle Garden and Ellis Island), 1820–1957* (Provo, UT: Ancestry.com, 2010), online database.

11. Andross, "Elder C. D. AcMoody," 23.

12. Frank S. Bond, "Fallen at the Battle's Front," *Review and Herald* 91, no. 54 (December 24, 1914): 12; E. E. Andross, "Fallen at His Post," Obituary, *Pacific Union Recorder* 14, no. 17 (November 26, 1914): 7.

13. Bond, "Fallen at the Battle's Front," 12; W. G. Bond, letter to W. A. Spicer, quoted in "Fallen at His Post," *Australasian Record* 19, no. 5 (February 1, 1915): 7; news note, *Review and Herald* 91, no. 50 (November 26, 1914): 24; *U.S., Consular Registration Certificates, 1907-1918* (Provo, UT: Ancestry.com Operations, 2013), online database. 1763–2002, Record Group 59. National Archives, Washington, DC.

14. Andross, "Fallen at His Post," 7.

CHAPTER 7

The Risks of Mission Labor in the Tropics: Southern Asia

The Southern Asia Division and its former territories are the resting places of many Adventist missionaries. Dores A. Robinson did not die alone.

Frederick W. Brown, who was a nurse, sailed for India on December 14, 1898, along with his wife, Katherine, who was a teacher, and their two children. They arrived in Calcutta (today's Kolkata) on February 9, 1899, where they joined the staff of the mission located at Bow Bazaar Street (pictured on the next page). In the summer, Fred and Katie were sent northwest to Ranchi, which is the capital of the state of Bihar. In the autumn, a smallpox epidemic broke out in Bihar. But the Brown family, along with Robinson and his wife, Edna, refused to leave the region, even though many Europeans did. Instead, they moved to Karmatar, where there was a small Adventist school and orphanage. The epidemic was raging with particular intensity here but with almost

Dores A. Robinson.

no medical care from Europeans. All four missionaries worked closely with the smallpox victims, and all four contracted the disease. Edna Robinson and Katie Brown both suffered but survived. Their husbands were not so fortunate.[1]

India Mission staff.

On December 21, 1899, Fred Brown passed away. He had been serving as a missionary in India for a little more than ten months. The

Dores A. and Edna Robinson in the early 1890s.

next month his former classmates at Battle Creek voted a resolution: "His life and death shall be to us an inspiration to continue steadfast in the work in which he has fallen, to bear the good tidings of salvation from sin and suffering to earth's needy ones."[2] A few days later, on December 29, Dores Robinson passed away too, having served in India for three years. Willie White wrote, "Overwork had unfitted him to battle with so dread a disease." Robinson's deputy, William Spicer, traveled from Calcutta; he later wrote, "I . . . was with him in his last conscious hours. I told him that if he must lay down his work, perhaps God would use that to draw attention to India's needs. . . . He replied with his swollen lips, 'Perhaps, perhaps

I hope.' " They were his last words and expressed his hope, a blessed hope, that the third angel's message would suffuse India. Brown and Robinson are buried in Karmatar; their graves lie side by side, along with that of a little orphan boy—one of those for whom they willingly gave their lives.[3]

Twenty-one years later, Eva Clements died in Rangoon. Her death in November 1920, after only seven months in the mission field, ended a bad two years for the Southern Asia Division, during which six church workers died. Like Eva Clements, Charles F. Lowry died in Rangoon but only twenty months before her. On September 18, 1916, Charles and his wife, Eva, and their two children arrived in Burma (also known today as Myanmar), where Charles, who had recently turned thirty, had been called as superintendent of the Burma Mission. In the words of W. W. Fletcher, who was the Southern Asia Division assistant secretary, the church leaders in India soon recognized "that in Brother Lowry we had a man of most devoted spirit and excellent judgment to lead out in the work there." His colleague in Burma, G. A. Hamilton, subsequently wrote ruefully: "His whole heart was in Burma. The people and their great need appealed to him very strongly. He willingly took the risks incidental to mission labor in the tropics, and paid the full price." Charles Lowry died on February 14, 1919, of smallpox. He had served as a missionary for not quite two and a half years.[4]

Dores Robinson's and Fred Brown's graves.

Six missionaries died in India in 1919 and 1920. They included Edith Bruce, who was a missionary nurse from America; she, at least, was a veteran missionary to India, having served there since 1908. She died on October 12, 1920, at the age of fifty-three. Her obituary paid a moving tribute, but one that is typical of how missionary deaths were regarded by fellow workers:

"We laid her to rest on the quiet slope of the lower ranges of the mighty Himalayas, until those ancient mountains shall catch the gleam of the bright morning when Jesus shall come to redeem from the grave the saints whose death is so precious in His sight, and whose last resting place He marks so tenderly."[5]

On top of these losses came the passing of Ernest Chapman; he died in January 1922 in his homeland of Australia after becoming fatally ill in India. Missionaries in Southern Asia saw his death as a continuation of the high death toll in 1919–1920, not least because it was likely that Chapman contracted tuberculosis in late 1920. Ernie and his wife, Elsie, both graduates of the Australasian Missionary College, had landed in India on November 9, 1920. He had been called to work in publishing, coordinating the translation and publication of Adventist literature into Indian languages, and then their sale by teams of local colporteurs. Elsie served as a Bible worker.[6]

Edith Bruce.

Ernest's assignment necessarily involved intensive effort, including venturing outside the relative comfort of the mission compounds, but he threw himself wholeheartedly into the work. This also entailed certain risks, however, but it seemed to have had an immediate missional impact. Yet there were personal health consequences. By July 1921, it was clear that Ernest had contracted a serious case of tuberculosis, which was complicated by unknown tropical fevers. The Chapmans were reassigned from Calicut, in southern India, to Bangalore, which, at an altitude of three thousand feet, was cooler and thought to have a better climate. But by the end of October 1921, Ernest was so ill that Elsie had to write his letters home for him.[7]

The church leaders were seriously concerned and decided to send the Chapmans back to Australia in the hope of effecting a cure. They traveled from Bangalore to Ceylon (now Sri Lanka), where they could take ship for Australia, without incident. They sailed from Colombo, Ceylon, for Australia on December 5, 1921, not quite thirteen months after their arrival in India. But this voyage taxed Ernest in his weakened condition. Rather than continuing on to his home city of Melbourne, as soon as the ship made landfall at Perth on December 16, he "was taken immediately to the Wooroloo Sanitorium [*sic*]." Ernest expressed the hope of returning to India once he was well. But it was already too late. "Several hemorrhages of the lungs" hastened his end. His last words were, "I just want a long sleep; I am very tired." Ernest Chapman passed away on January 6, 1922. He was twenty-six years old. His service in India lasted one year and one month.[8]

His death marked the end of a particularly lethal period for Adventist mission in Southern Asia. How deadly had the years 1919 and 1920 been? There were 110 Adventist foreign missionaries in India and Burma. This meant that the average annual mortality rate among Adventist missionaries in these two years (disregarding Chapman, who died later) was equivalent to 54.5 deaths per thousand. If one looks at studies by historical demographers, this mortality rate contrasts sharply with that of Westerners in general: even in 1919, "when influenza prevailed" in India, the rate was 25.5 deaths per thousand. In other words, it was more than twice as dangerous for Adventist missionaries in India as for Westerners in general.[9]

―――――――

The years of 1919 and 1920 had been, no doubt, especially bad years. But this statistic highlights how dangerous mission service could be. As medicine and public hygiene improved, Adventist missionaries' life expectancy while in the Southern Asia mission field increased. Yet today's nations of Burma, India, Pakistan, and Sri Lanka remained places where there were much greater risks of serious illness and premature death than other mission fields.

In 1909, a young graduate of the Southern Training School (now Southern Adventist University) and his wife accepted a call to serve as missionaries in India. Gentry G. Lowry was twenty-five, and Bertha, his wife, was twenty-three. India must have seemed an utterly strange land to a young couple from the countryside of Tennessee, and its culture alien—yet they loved India. They gave their lives to India. In 1914, G. G. Lowry established the South India Training School—the ancestor of today's Spicer Adventist University. From 1918 to 1936,

Lowry worked across the Southern Asia Division, serving sequentially as the superintendent of several unions, including Burma, where his brother Charles had died in 1919. He developed a reputation as a skillful and capable Christian leader. Furthermore, he was known for what a colleague humorously called "the gift of tongues, supplemented by earnest study." Over the years, Lowry became "proficient in Tamil, Malayalam, Telugu, Kanarese, and Urdu, and also conversed and preached in Hindi and Bengali."[10]

While he was the superintendent of the Northeast India Mission in the mid-1930s, however, he started to have health problems that became increasingly severe. They had started in 1933 when he had needed surgery for appendicitis. Complications had followed, and he suffered from chronic abdominal pain. Another surgery took place in 1935, but the pain continued, and doctors warned that he needed treatment in a hospital in Britain or the United States. They also warned him that India's climate was bad for his health and that he should not return.

Bertha and Gentry Lowry at a camp meeting in Tennessee, early in 1909.

On March 22, 1936, the Southern Asia Division committee voted to send Lowry home for surgery, with the expectation that he would not return. A few days later he, his wife, and his younger son, Roscoe, were at the train station in Ranchi. An Indian pastor, Jonas Singh, was one of many who came to see him off. Pastor Singh later remembered that he fought back tears as he said goodbye to Gentry, Bertha, and Roscoe.

"I will see you in heaven, Lowry Sahib," he said, addressing Lowry with an Indian title that indicated respect.

Pastor Singh never forgot his astonishment when Gentry replied, "No, Brother, I will see you next year. God has His plans for this church in India, and I believe I am part of them. And if so, He will spare my life long enough to do what I need to do."[11]

Lowry went home and had the surgery; true to his word, he returned to India in 1937. In 1941, he was elected president of the Southern Asia Division. He soon faced immense challenges: the Imperial Japanese Army overran Burma early in 1942, while the fleets of the Imperial Japanese Navy attacked ports in both Ceylon and India. Adventist missionaries had to be evacuated from Burma under difficult conditions—Eric B. Hare among them—and the challenges of operating in a war zone had to be met. As a colleague wrote after Lowry's death, "The wartime dangers that threatened and seemed to be scattering the lifetime work of our brother were a great burden on his heart and mind. . . . The results of nearly fifty years of labor and giving, and the lives of many workers, were in jeopardy. Momentous decisions had to be made. Uncertainty and anxiety were in the air. It was in the midst of the hottest season . . . experienced for fifty years."[12]

After years of dedicated service in Southern Asia, Lowry's health was not robust, and the impact of immense stress on a weakened constitution was fatal. On May 2, 1942, Gentry Lowry suffered a stroke, and he died two days later on May 4.

Gentry Lowry in June 1941.

Believing that the conditions in India were affecting his health, church leaders offered him the chance, even encouraged him, to return permanently to his "homeland"—the United States. This gave the prospect of preserving his life. Instead, in the words of Isaiah, G. G. Lowry "poured out his soul unto death" (Isaiah 53:12, KJV). India had become his home. Sharing the good news in Southern Asia was his passion. When he passed away, he was not yet fifty-eight years old.

Robert A. Beckner left America in 1908, aged just twenty-two, and went as a missionary to Burma. Two years later, he married Mabelle McMoran, an American expatriate, and he served in Burma until 1923, when Mabelle's serious illness forced them to make a permanent return. Sadly, she died in the Melrose Sanitarium, near Boston, on June 16, 1923. A year later Robert married Ethel May, who went with him when he returned to Burma. They served seventeen years in Southern Asia, where two sons and three daughters were born. Apart from a brief stint at the Oriental Watchman Publishing House in Poona (Pune, today) in India, Robert, Ethel, and their children mostly engaged in frontline mission work in rugged and disease-ridden areas. As Roy Cottrell, a fellow missionary to Burma, put it, "Without any of the conveniences of modern life, they labored uncomplainingly and happily for the Burmese and the Karens." But these endeavors took a toll in the form of ill-defined fevers, amoebic dysentery, and other ailments. When the family took a furlough in 1933–1934, for instance, they were all found "to have the Ameba parasites," while the oldest son (seven) had worms, and Ethel was anemic.[13]

Toward the end of the 1930s, as Cottrell later recalled, Beckner "realized that his physical powers were weakening; yet he labored faithfully on, taking long, perilous jungle trips, when the strain must have told heavily on his already-failing vitality." Robert himself recorded in November 1940: "This past year I have found myself without much endurance and easily subject to fever. . . . The doctors feared I would not pull through." In a letter to his family in America, he describes in gruesome detail how, over several months, sores (a regular hazard in the jungle) stopped healing. They might leak "a great deal of bad blood" with "a great deal of puss discharged"; doctors drained "a lot of pussy blood, but still infection proceeded." Cottrell described how "the many prayers of the . . . native believers, who loved him so well, ascended to God, and his life was spared." But this lasted only long enough for the Beckners to finally return to the United States, after Robert had spent thirty-two years in Southern Asia. He returned with chronic appendicitis, chronic enteritis, and septicemia. Sadly, nothing could be done, even at the Glendale Sanitarium in California, to effect a cure, and Robert died there on April 23, 1941, just a month after arriving back in the States.[14]

Robert was only fifty-four, yet he was worn out by arduous service and, like D. A. Robinson and G. G. Lowry, by overwork. Ethel was left a widow with five children. A. W. Cormack, an associate secretary of the General Conference, wrote to her: "in an effort to express very imperfectly the deep sympathy that we feel for you and your loved ones in this sad hour of trial through which you are passing." He urged her, "Don't give room in your thinking to doubts and questionings why these things are permitted or how they could be allowed to happen. . . . Not now but when the mists have rolled away will you in the kingdom with Brother Beckner be able to see that in some strange way this experience has been blessed of God to the family and to the children, and in the saving of souls." We see again the familiar blending of attempted consolation and inspiration to further work to save souls. It was rhetoric with which Robert Beckner would, however, undoubtedly have agreed wholeheartedly.[15]

Thus, even after modern hospitals, medicine, and hygiene became more widespread, going as a missionary to India, Ceylon, or Burma still meant accepting a much greater danger of early death than if one remained in one's Western homelands. In many mission fields, there continued to be, at least until World War II, a very real risk to the missionary of being buried in some foreign field, far from family and home.

1. D. A. Robinson, "Calcutta, India," *Review and Herald* 76, no. 15 (April 11, 1899): 12; F. W. Brown, "Northwestern India," *Review and Herald* 76, no. 43 (October 24, 1899): 14; W. C. W[hite], "Obituary," *Union Conference Record* [*Australasian Record*] 3, no. 3 (March 1, 1900): 16; W. A. Spicer, "Some Facts About Early Work in India," *Eastern Tidings* 36, no. 9A (May 8, 1941): 6.

2. Resolution of the American Medical Missionary College, Class of 1901, quoted in U[riah] S[mith], "In Light of the Promises," *Review and Herald* 77, no. 3 (January 16, 1900): 42.

3. White, "Obituary," 16; Spicer, "Some Facts About Early Work," 6; A. T. Robinson, quoted in "A Message From India," *Bible Echo* 15, no. 10 (March 5, 1900): 159.

4. W. W. Fletcher, "Death of Elder Charles F. Lowry," *Review and Herald* 96, no. 19 (May 8, 1919): 22; G. A. Hamilton, "Lowry," Obituaries, *Review and Herald* 96, no. 21 (May 22, 1919): 31.

5. W. W. Fletcher, "Death of Sister Edith Bruce," *Review and Herald* 98, no. 3 (January 20, 1921): 25, 26.

6. W. W. Fletcher, "Condensed Quadrennial Report of the Southern Asia Division," *Eastern Tidings* 17, no. 13 (July 1, 1922): 6; W. W. Fletcher, "New Workers Expected," *Eastern Tidings* 15, no. 18 (September 15, 1920): 6; R. H. Constandt, "Chapman," Obituaries, *Australasian Record* 26, no. 3 (February 6, 1922): 7; Reuben E. Hare, "Chapman," *Australasian Record* 49, no. 12 (March 19, 1945): 7.

7. Constandt, "Chapman," 7; Mrs. Ernest Chapman, quoted in *Australasian Record* 25, no. 21 (October 17, 1921): 8; "A Request for Prayer," *Australasian Record* 26, no. 1 (January 9, 1922): 6, 7.

8. W. G. Turner, "Secretary's Report," *Australasian Record* 26, no. 22 (October 9, 1922): 9; "News Notes," *Eastern Tidings* 17, no. 2 (January 15, 1922): 15; "Death of Brother Ernest Chapman," *Eastern Tidings*, January 15, 1922, 16; "A Request for Prayer," 6; Constandt, "Chapman," 7; H. E. Piper, quoted in "The Death of Brother Ernest Chapman," *Eastern Tidings* 17, no. 11 (June 1, 1922): 5, 6.

9. See General Conference of Seventh-day Adventists, *Year Book of the Seventh-day Adventist Denomination, 1920* (Washington, DC: Review and Herald®, 1920), 272–277; Ira Klein, "Death in India, 1871–1921," *Journal of Asian Studies* 32, no. 4 (August 1973): 643.

10. R. B. Thurber, "Gentry G. Lowry," Journey's End, *Review and Herald* 119, no. 31 (July 30, 1942): 22.

11. This story was later told to the author's father, who passed it on to the author.

12. Thurber, "Gentry G. Lowry," 22, 23.

13. Roy F. Cottrell, "Robert A. Beckner," Journey's End, *Review and Herald* 118, no. 39 (July 31, 1941): 23; P. F. Bicknell, "Mrs. Mabelle D. Beckner," Obituaries, *Review and Herald* 100, no. 28 (July 12, 1923): 22; medical reports and correspondence, Beckner Appointee file, GCA, Record Group 21, file no. 45216.

14. Cottrell, "Beckner," 23. Robert A. Beckner to E. D. Dick, November 1, 1940; Robert A. Beckner to "Folks," September 9, 1940; Beckners' "Information on Returning Missionaries" form, October 15, 1941, GCA, Record Group 21, file no. 45216.

15. A. W. Cormack to Mrs. Robert Beckner, April 29, 1941, GCA, Record Group 21, file no. 45216.

CHAPTER 8

Paying the Price

We have surveyed the mission fields of the Seventh-day Adventist Church from the 1890s to the 1920s, with a brief excursion forward to the 1940s in India. We have seen, time and time again, that young men and women went out as missionaries and that far too many died quickly, often within a year of arriving in the mission field. Today, "international service employees"—the church's current name for missionaries—sign up for a five-year term of service. As we have seen, very few missionaries in the quarter century we have focused on made it to five years because they died. At first glance, their level of commitment and their degree of sacrifice were extraordinary. Indeed, in some areas at some moments in history (especially in Southern Asia immediately after World War I), the Adventist mortality rate for missionaries was shockingly high.

This fact raises questions that must be addressed: While individual stories are moving, how indicative are they of broader trends? How typical were the experiences described so far for Seventh-day Adventist missionaries? How many, to borrow the words of Abraham Lincoln, "gave the last full measure of devotion"?[1] How many had to pay the supreme price—"the price of victory," as William Spicer put it?[2]

The following statistics are taken from records kept by the General Conference Statistical Secretary up to 1973 and then by the Office of Archives and Statistics (since 2011, the Office of Archives, Statistics, and Research). They provide sobering insight into the self-sacrificial commitment of our Adventist forebears.

We often tell stories of the very first pioneers, stressing their heroism and resolution. Unfortunately, this emphasis means that, almost by default, we imply that they were unusually steadfast. While we should certainly applaud their spirit of sacrifice, the truth is that it was not just the famous pioneers who were remarkably selfless in the cause of the three angels' messages. What is exceptional is how widespread self-lessness was and how far down it spread into the ranks of what we might be tempted to call "ordinary church members," were it not for how extraordinarily willing they were to pay any price to proclaim prophetic truths and the good news of a risen Savior ministering in the heavenly sanctuary.

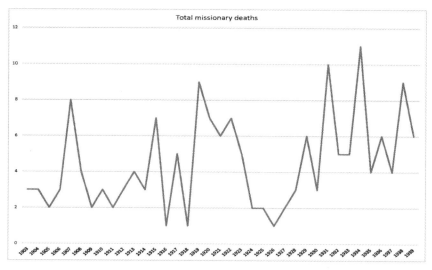

Figure 1.

We can see from figure 1 the annual number of missionary deaths in the mission field from 1903 through 1939, when World War II began. It is not only the missionaries' spirit of sacrifice that is striking, but also the fact that Seventh-day Adventists were not deterred from taking the place of deceased missionaries despite the death toll. In other words, if some Adventists were daunted by the high casualty rates of missionaries, there were always enough volunteers to replenish the ranks of the fallen. And missionaries themselves kept urging others to supplement their ranks and take their places. The words of Sarah Mareta Young, which were quoted earlier, written in a letter to friends just weeks before her death, were far from exceptional: "May many more be found who are ready to say, 'Here am I, send me.'"[3]

Figure 2 plots the numbers of new missionaries sent out every year for most of the first forty years of the twentieth century. Until the 1970s, the church's official metric for missionaries was not the number "in service" in mission fields but the numbers dispatched from the North American, European, and Australasian homelands to mission fields. It is this key statistic that is charted in figure 2. The numbers of new missionaries going out always exceeded the number of deaths. In the first four decades of the twentieth century, up to the start of World War II, the Seventh-day Adventist Church formally called and dispatched 4,591 missionaries. Because the official statistics do not always include spouses (much less children), the actual number who went to foreign mission fields would have been higher. There were always more men and women—mostly young men and women—willing to go throughout the pre–World War I period, even though going as a missionary meant a high chance of not returning.

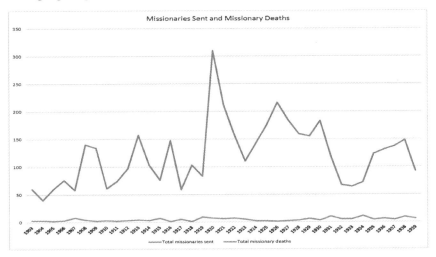

Figure 2.

While we should admire the willingness and the selflessness underpinning the bare statistics, let us not understate what these men and women from the mission heartlands of North America, Western Europe, southern Africa, and Australasia were signing up for. Just what were the odds that foreign mission service might prove fatal? Figure 3, on the next page, powerfully brings home the fact that the annual death toll, calculated as deaths per hundred new missionaries sent each year, was considerable. Earlier, we noted the appalling mortality rate of Adventist missionaries in Southern Asia after World War I; it was unusually bad. But the death toll among Adventist missionaries in general up to World War II was such that no one could be sanguine about going as a foreign missionary.

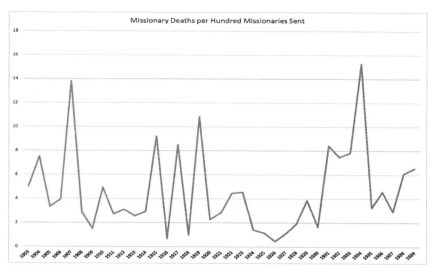

Figure 3.

Yet committed men and women still volunteered, they still went to the mission field, and they remained there, often for many years—a point we will return to later. But let us pause for a moment and reflect on a profound and humbling point: these men and women went as missionaries, *knowing* that it easily could be a death sentence.

The exact statistics would not have been known, but Adventists knew very well the risk of mission service. Much of the information and many of the quotations in this book come from reports of missionary deaths, written by colleagues soon after they passed away, and published in the church magazines in the mission homelands. While overseas mission service was sanitized to some extent in church publications in the second half of the twentieth century, in the first decades of the century, every Seventh-day Adventist grew up reading stories of the sacrifices, the suffering, and the early deaths of those working in foreign mission fields.

In fact, if one goes through the issues of the *Australasian Record* that precede the March 9, 1920, issue, in which is printed the brief notice that Eva May Clements has been called to the Southern Asia Division, they contain stories about Australian missionaries to India who had just arrived home, were very ill, and were being treated for tuberculosis and typhoid. Around the same time, the stories of the deaths of Norman Wiles and Pearl Tolhurst were being printed.

Additionally, the reports in church papers, extended families, and networks of friends from the academies and colleges, influenced a high proportion of Adventist young people. Many Seventh-day Adventists in the "homelands" would have known of a relative, friend, or friend of a friend who had died in a mission field; they could put a name, or perhaps even a face, to the sacrifice.

In spite of this knowledge of the costs, Seventh-day Adventists, especially young people, were inspired to serve. In 1907, William Spicer, a General Conference secretary, described the death of two missionaries, the reactions of their colleagues and loved ones, and of how "even amid sorrow, the word of courage is spoken, lest any should hold back from service." The truth of this is evident from the stories of sacrifice told in the previous chapters. But Spicer continues, "The Lord has in preparation, somewhere, the workers who are to step in and fill up the ranks."[4] This was not mere rhetoric. Spicer was right: there were always workers who would step in and fill the ranks of the fallen.

And at times, these missionaries were conscious that they were stepping into the shoes of the deceased. For example, the summer after Christian Wunderlich's death, German Union leaders publicly announced at a camp meeting in Friedensau that they needed "one additional worker to go out and join the East African Mission." A visiting American church leader related the response: "On the instant, volunteers were springing to their feet in all parts of the great tent, and the union committee had seventeen earnest candidates from whom to select their missionary. These young people have a very stern reminder, too, of the fact that volunteering for East Africa is no light matter. Just on the edge of the sanitarium grounds . . . a stone marks the resting-place of Brother Wunderlich . . . who went out to Africa . . . and who returned stricken with death."[5]

Nearly twenty years later, it is striking that, despite the reports of disease and death being printed in the *Australasian Record*, young Adventists in Australia and New Zealand did not stop volunteering for mission service. Instead, as a church leader reflected with both pride and humility, "The sacrifice of these lives has brought a new inspiration to many of our young people, and they have sought to take up the burden laid down by others."[6]

From North America, southern Africa, Western and Central Europe, and Australasia—and increasingly from the mission fields too—men and women went as missionaries. There was a steady stream of new recruits, ready and willing to endanger their earthly lives, because eternal life beckoned. They wanted people of "all nations, tribes . . . and tongues" to be with them among the "great multitude . . . standing before the throne and before the Lamb" at the end of time and abiding "before the throne of God" forever. And God would "wipe away every tear from their eyes" (Revelation 7:9, 15, 17). With this promise of consolation for the sorrows of this world and the prospect of sharing the good news of life everlasting, there were always enough Adventists ready to risk their all.

The public-health situation started to improve after World War I as measures for sanitation and hygiene began to be widely adopted. Missionaries' health improved markedly after World War II because of the introduction of antibiotics, the further expansion of hospitals and public-hygiene programs, and the coming of better transportation links, especially by air, so that fewer missionaries were left utterly isolated. Yet there were still some Adventist mission stations in Africa that could not be reached without weeks of travel until the end of the 1950s.[7]

While many dangers decreased, they did not disappear. As "civilization" spread, so did its vices, and the spread of new travel technology brought new hazards too. In a twelve-month period in 1946 and 1947, for example, the Central American Union had four missionaries leave or die. In 1947, they were obliged "to send one of their teachers home because of immoral conduct," and another made an early return after he was attacked, beaten, and robbed. The violent assault followed not long after the tragic deaths of the union president, Noel Kinzer, and the education department secretary, Harry Larrabee, who both died in a plane crash in April 1946. Noel Kinzer's widow, Vivian, wrote to the General Conference associate secretary who was responsible for missionary recruitment and liaison in the Inter-American Division. She said she and her fourteen-year-old son (who had been born while they were in Central America) were going through a "dark and trying time." She continued, "My husband's tragic death was a terrible shock to me. It is so hard to understand why the Lord permitted such a dreadful thing to happen." And yet, she concluded, "We are determined as never before to consecrate ourselves to the work of God and do all we can to hasten the Lord's coming. . . . I want to serve in the Lord's work where I can be of most service." The spirit of sacrifice was still strong.[8]

As mentioned earlier, serving as a missionary, while never completely secure, became safer in the years after World War II. And so, this narrative of sacrifice does not continue past the midpoint of the twentieth century. Lives were lost and sacrifices were made, including those of being far from families and friends, about which more will be said in chapters 10 and 11. There was and is, however, an important difference to the pre–World War II situation. While missionaries in the second half of the twentieth century and early twenty-first century knew that serious disease or death, whether for themselves or their family members, could not be ruled out, it was a remote possibility.

During the first half of the twentieth century, in contrast, death was an outcome that Adventist missionaries to Africa, Latin America, the Caribbean, the Middle East, Asia, and the South Pacific, knew was entirely possible. Indeed, as we have seen, dying in the field or contracting a fatal disease was likely in certain areas—and after a very short time, at that. Going as a missionary involved a strong chance of offering one's life as a sacrifice.

Why did so many Adventist missionaries die? As we have seen in chapters 6 and 7, overwork was undoubtedly a factor. The urgency Adventists feel about their mission due to the soon return of Christ means that many Seventh-day Adventist leaders have been workaholics and died early as a result (starting with James White!). But as we have also seen, it was not just ministers and administrators alone who died—spouses and secretaries, teachers and nurses, and children also died. Overwork alone cannot explain their deaths.

In fact, the chief reason for the high death toll among Adventist missionaries of the late-nineteenth and early twentieth centuries is that they did not remain in enclaves or institutions. Instead, they got out and got their hands dirty. They worked for the local people and among those people.

Many Westerners, even missionaries, influenced by racism, tried to seclude themselves as much as possible from local populations. Seventh-day Adventists wanted to be among the people as much as possible so that they could emulate the teaching and healing ministry of Jesus. Consequently, they were exposed to disease and dangerous situations, and so they died. They died because they wanted to tell people of their Savior. They offered their lives as sacrifices.

1. Abraham Lincoln, "Gettysburg Address," November 19, 1863, Gettysburg, PA.

2. W. A. S[picer], "The Price of Victory," *Review and Herald* 83, no. 3 (January 18, 1906): 5, 6.

3. Sarah Mareta Young, quoted in *Union Conference Record* [*Australasian Record*] 10, no. 17 (August 20, 1906): 12.

4. W. A. S[picer], "Two Vacant Places in the Mission Field Ranks," *Review and Herald* 84, no. 9 (Febuary 28, 1907): 5.

5. W. A. S[picer], "Young Germany Responds," *Review and Herald* 83, no. 35 (August 30, 1906): 5.

6. W. G. Turner, "Secretary's Report," *Australasian Record* 26, no. 22 (October 9, 1922): 9.

7. Robert Lemon (former General Conference treasurer), discussion with the author, 2013; see also Yvonne Davy, *Going With God on Missions of Mercy in Central Africa* (Washington, DC: Review and Herald®, 1959).

8. Mrs. N. H. Kinder to T. J. Michael, June 18, 1946, Kinzer appointee file, GCA, Record Group 21, file no. 46213.

PART 3
Living

CHAPTER 9

Life Giving

L et us now pass from death into life. Even if a missionary did not pay the ultimate price, leaving behind loved ones and one's homeland was a sacrifice. While the risk of mortality had decreased after World War I, discomfort and illness were likely, and separation from all one had held dear was certain. But for the Great Commission to be fulfilled, it could not be otherwise. Milton Kern, the founder of the Young People's Missionary Volunteer movement, wrote an appeal for new foreign missionaries in 1930: "The Master did not say, 'Go preach the gospel in countries of the temperate zone where there are few insect pests, where the altitude is not very high, and where you will have good beds and all the conveniences of civilization.' His last command on earth to His followers was, 'Go ye into all the world, and preach the gospel to every creature.' " Writing to Kern five years later, Robert H. Pierson, who eventually spent twenty-five years as a missionary in three divisions, put it well: mission service required "a willingness to sacrifice friends, loved ones, and comforts of life."[1] While this can still be the case today, how much truer was it before jet travel, widespread air conditioning and refrigeration, and modern medicine and hygiene!

Robert H. Pierson as a young man. He submitted this photo with his application for missionary service.

Being a missionary could thus be a life sentence as well as a death sentence. For it was not just the missionaries who died who gave their lives; so did many of those who lived, though in a different sense. As a Chinese pastor wrote of Ezra Longway, who served in the Far East for fifty-five years (and who we will return to in chapter 10), the missionary "not only gave his money, talents and energy but he gave his life to us."[2]

In this, Adventist missionaries were following in the footsteps of the pioneers of faith, forging the latest links in a chain of faithfulness that goes back to biblical times. The author of Hebrews, in his great narrative of sacred history and the people of faith (Hebrews 11:1–12:2), left a historical record of the march of God's people down through the corridors of time. Hebrews 11 tells us that some of God's people "were tortured, not accepting deliverance. . . . Still others had trial of mockings and scourgings, yes, and of chains and imprisonment. They were stoned, they were sawn in two, . . . were slain with the sword" (verses 35–37). But not all of these heroes of the faith perished. Others, we are told, "wandered about in sheepskins and goatskins, being destitute, afflicted, tormented—of whom the world was not worthy" (verses 37, 38). In other words, some died for their faith, but others lived and experienced deprivation, danger, and distress for their faith.

In Adventist history, our missionaries "wandered" and suffered. They rarely were tortured or killed, but as we have seen, many died, and all forfeited family connections, comforts, and opportunities for personal or professional betterment in exchange for lives of service. These are extraordinary men and women—the creators of our worldwide church "of whom" we are "not worthy."

While it is right to acknowledge what these missionaries achieved and what they sacrificed, we should not stress their extraordinary qualities too much, lest we undermine the chief lesson they would undoubtedly want us to learn and apply in our own lives. For they were, all of them, flawed and imperfect human beings, transformed by the power of the Holy Spirit. Rather than feeling that we have nothing in common with them, their examples can inspire us precisely because they were quite ordinary men and women—and often very young men and women. They were willing to trust in God and also were willing to pay the ultimate price.

There are countless stories of their heroism, triumph, and tragedy, though, sadly, many have been forgotten. But we can be inspired not just by the missionaries who were "faithful unto death" (Revelation

2:10, KJV). We should also be inspired by hundreds of other Adventist missionaries who did not die in service but, instead, served for decades in foreign lands. They, too, offered up themselves as living sacrifices, giving their lives in a different sense. Whereas some gave their lives *for* the people of races and nations not their own, other missionaries gave their lives *to* peoples in faraway places. Like the flawed heroes described by the author of Hebrews, many Adventist missionaries abandoned their homelands and spent much of their lives as "foreigners and strangers on earth. . . . If they had been thinking of the country they had left, they would have had opportunity to return. Instead, they were longing for a better country—a heavenly one" (Hebrews 11:13, 15, 16, NIV).

By 1950, the Seventh-day Adventist Church had sent out more than six thousand missionaries. In surveying their life histories, I find myself in the same position as the author of Hebrews: "And what more shall I say? I do not have time to tell about" all those who, by their heroic self-sacrifice and remarkable commitment to the people of their adopted homelands, built up a North American, European, and Australasian denomination into a worldwide movement (verse 32, NIV).

Just a few examples will have to suffice.

The next chapter tells the stories of missionaries who served long term—case studies in living sacrifice. Because they survived and appear in church records for many years, we know more about them than about the men and women whose stories I have told thus far. Most gave decades of their lives to countries far from those "they had left" because they earnestly wanted their fellow human beings to know about the heavenly country.

In summarizing their lives of service and selflessness, I intend to illustrate broader trends, outline their typical experiences, and inspire similar enthusiasm for service. In selecting particular stories of missionaries, I do not mean to imply they were in some way superior. Many other missionaries were as steadfast and self-sacrificing as those I have singled out. Like Eva Clements, however, the men and women we will meet in the next chapter stand for hundreds of other missionaries—many of whose lives remain largely obscured. Their stories give a sense of what it was like to serve in the mission field in the first half of the twentieth century.

These stories also illustrate another broader point: we are interdependent in the Seventh-day Adventist Church because there is no part of the world field that has not given its sons and daughters to other parts of the world. And every continent and world division has benefited in some way from the benevolence of other parts of the world. That generosity has frequently been financial in form. But often it has been in the shape of a more precious resource than money: the lives spent in ministry to brothers and sisters in other countries, emulating the incarnational ministry of Jesus Christ.

---

1. M. E. Kern, "Urgent Calls for Missionary Doctors," *Review and Herald* 107, no. 51 (October 2, 1930): 32; Robert H. Pierson to M. E. Kern, March 17, 1935, Pierson appointee file, GCA, Record Group 21, file no. 4853.

2. Samuel Young, "Reflections on Elder Longway's Life," October 1, 1987, Longway appointee file, GCA, Record Group 21, file no. 5842.

CHAPTER 10

"Unusual Sacrifice":
The Far East and Pacific

In July 1903, Dr. Arthur C. Selmon and Dr. Bertha Loveland, two physicians, were married. Just a few months later, they sailed from the United States as missionaries. Born within eleven days of each other, they were both just twenty-five years of age. Arthur and Bertha "spent twenty-one years as . . . missionaries in China," as a colleague wrote when Arthur passed away, adding that they "rendered excellent service in that field, and the Lord blessed their labors to the relief of much physical suffering and to the salvation of souls." In addition to being a physician, Arthur Selmon was also a minister; as noted earlier, he conducted the funeral service for Maude Miller. Dr. Selmon was driven by a deep desire to save souls, and we will come back to this point.

Although Dr. Selmon did not die in China, he still had a price to pay when he returned home. The hard years had taken their toll on him and, in 1931, at just fifty-three years of age he died of heart disease. His heart had probably been weakened by a bout of rheumatic fever he had suffered earlier in China. Although he did not die there, he still had to pay a price on his return home. [1]

The twenty-one-year term of service of the two Doctors Selmon was not exceptional—far from it. Ezra Longway's fifty-five years in the Far Eastern Division, with thirty of those years in China, may be the record for foreign service as a Seventh-day Adventist missionary. He and his wife, Inez, were called to Thailand in 1918. They served for three years in Southeast Asia, where a daughter, Eva, was born. The family was called to China in 1922. Four were missionaries there for the next forty years. Four more children were born during this time: Myrtle, Delbert, Ralph, and David. [2]

Ezra Longway stayed in China throughout World War II. The majority of Adventist missionaries were evacuated to other countries in

1940 or 1941, including Inez, Ralph, and David, but Ezra remained. He was joined by a handful of other Adventists who served in the very basic China Division headquarters in Chongqing. (George Appel, who will be discussed later, was among those who stayed.) They supervised as best as they could the work of Chinese pastors and nurses, and a number of missionaries who were in the western provinces and remained (including the Warrens, who will be discussed later). All those who stayed were to experience danger and deprivation. But it

Ezra, Eva, Myrtle, and Inez Longway. This was a passport photo from 1922.

was worse for the Longway family. The older three children were in the United States for their education, but Inez, Ralph (who was fourteen), and David (ten) were caught up in the Japanese invasion, having been evacuated to the Philippines. They were interned in "the infamous Baguio prisoner-of-war camp in the mountains near Manila" until 1945. Later, a senior church leader wrote to "recognize the unusual sacrifice you and Mrs. Longway made through the years of World War II."[3]

A convoy of trucks about to depart Shanghai for Chongqing, which is just over a thousand miles by road.

Yet even after these experiences, the Longways remained committed to their service in East Asia. After the Communist victory in the Chinese Civil War, the Longways moved to Hong Kong to the newly created South China Island Union Mission. Ezra's experience was vital for the new church entity, which covered Hong Kong, Macao, and Taiwan. These three political areas had never before been in the same church organizational unit and had limited denominational infrastructure because the strongholds of the church in China had been elsewhere. After twelve years of helping the union to form a firm foundation, including establishing several new institutions, Ezra was elected as the field secretary of the Far Eastern Division in 1963, a post he held for the next eleven years, though the Longways continued to be based in Hong Kong. Inez died in 1973; later that year Ezra married Florence Winton. In early 1974, at the age of seventy-eight, Ezra retired with Florence.[4]

Much more could be said about the Longways, but I have summarized Ezra's career because it could be seen as abnormal and atypical and thus not indicative of broader trends. While his foreign mission service of fifty-five years truly was exceptional, decades of dedicated service were, if never ordinary, still far from extraordinary. A few examples will illustrate this point.

Merritt and Wilma Warren went with their baby daughter Helen to China in 1913, when Merritt was twenty-two and Wilma was twenty-four. Merritt and Wilma served in Chinese territories for thirty-six years until 1949. With the China Division in disarray and Merritt approaching sixty years of age, he was urged by the division president "to return to . . . [his] homeland" because he had "given all that can be expected." It was true; for instance, Merritt had hiked, he believed, twenty-five thousand miles in his decades in China, including a thousand miles in the spring and summer of 1931 when he and another missionary, Claude Miller, had traveled on foot together "in bandit-infested areas in West China as they visited . . . believers under extremely difficult circumstances."[5]

In many other ways, however, the Warrens had given their all. Like the Longways, the Warrens remained in China throughout World War II, suffering the same hazards and hardships as the Chinese people. During their nearly four decades of mission service, they enjoyed four furloughs to the United States, but they always returned to China.

Meanwhile, they sent their six children to boarding academies and colleges in America, which meant missing many of their formative years, all but one of their high-school and college graduations, and the weddings of all three daughters. In a sense, they not only gave their lives to China, but they also gave up their children's lives, for their children did not grow up with them. Merritt and Wilma did what they thought was best for their children, and they may have been right. Yet this does not lessen the sacrifice they made—one that was typical of many missionaries.

After all they had sacrificed, instead of accepting retirement, Merritt asked, "Brethren, isn't there some field in the Far Eastern Division I can serve?" Warren, a former union president in China, was called "to serve as president of the East Visayan Mission in the Philippines." He accepted this call, for he was willing, like other missionaries (as we will see later), to accept what some might see as a demotion in order to continue in mission service. Warren distinguished himself there and after two years was elected president of the North Philippine Union. He spent six years in the Philippines, serving with grace and good humor. Subsequently, the Warrens returned to the Chinese mission work they loved, serving five more years in Taiwan. They retired to California in 1960, when Merritt was sixty-nine and Wilma was seventy-two. The following photographs show the Warrens as they were in 1913, when first traveling to China, and then decades later, as Merritt Warren was closer to retiring. The years of toil are engraved on Merritt's features. Yet as the Warrens looked back over years of privation, isolation, joy, sorrow, souls influenced, and souls won, Merritt and Wilma were in no doubt about the character of their experience: "Hasn't the Lord been good to us all through the years?"[6]

Merritt and Wilma Warren, photographed in 1913, the year they first went to China.

Merritt Warren with Gil de Guzman, the president of the South Philippine Union, and W. E. Nelson, a touring General Conference field secretary, in 1953.

Warren, Guzman, and Nelson with missionary and national workers at Mountain View College.

George and Laura Appel went to the Far East in October 1920, when he was twenty-eight and she was twenty-seven years old. George and Laura spent "the next 38 years . . . in mission service." They labored for twenty-nine years in Singapore, Borneo, the Philippines, and China;

George Appel in the Philippines in July 1926.

George was a key administrator in the North China and Northwest China Unions and "was also actively involved in pioneer work in Mongolia and Tibet." The younger of their two sons, Alva, was born in Singapore. For the relatives of the Appels, as was the case with other families of missionaries, being distant and cut off from seeing their grandchildren and nephews grow up was a hardship. This situation was only partly ameliorated by letters and photographs sent in the mail, but they often took many weeks to arrive.[7]

The Appels experienced trials in addition to separation. They saw tragedy firsthand: George worked closely with Elmer Coulston, and Laura Appel and Leatha Coulston struck up a firm and lasting friendship that endured past Elmer's death. George also witnessed a number of other missionary deaths. The Appels, furthermore, were another family that continued their mission service in China during World War II. George filled the difficult wartime role of secretary-treasurer of the China Division, working with Ezra Longway, the acting president.

A portrait of the whole Appel family—George, Laura, Melvin, and Alva—was taken in China to send to relatives for Christmas 1929.

After twenty-nine years in the Far Eastern and China Divisions, George was elected as the first president of the Middle East Division in 1950, and George and Laura spent another eight years in foreign

mission service, based in Lebanon, before eventually retiring after nearly four decades as missionaries.[8]

In each of the three cases highlighted in this chapter—the Longways, Warrens, and Appels—the missionaries eventually retired in North America; while the language used was that they were going "home," the truth is that their homes were elsewhere. The supposed homelands to which they were returning must have felt, in many ways, very alien.

George Appel in Lebanon in the 1950s.

Moving now from the Middle East, China, and Southeast Asia, we also find examples of extraordinary long-term commitment to the South Pacific. George L. and Maybelle H. Sterling were missionaries from America who replaced the Australians Albert and Hettie Piper in the Cook Islands. Both George and Maybelle survived; indeed, they lived to a ripe old age and avoided the fate of Julia Caldwell, Sarah Mareta Young, and Hettie Piper. But the Sterlings embody a hard truth: those who blazed a trail sharing the third angel's message often had to endure physical discomfort and culture shock as well as disease and isolation from friends and loved ones.[9]

In June 1908, Maybelle Klopfenstein married George Sterling, a young colporteur and part-time assistant evangelist from Michigan. Within four weeks of their marriage, they left as missionaries, sailing from San Francisco to the Society Islands in the South Pacific. The archipelago is best known for its largest island, Tahiti, and is part of French Polynesia. Today, the region is a vacation destination, but in the early 1900s, when George and Maybelle served there, the isles of the South Pacific were still remote and fever ridden. Westerners often died or contracted fatal illnesses, and as we have seen, this included Adventist missionaries. But Maybelle and George served for three decades in island mission fields without long-term ill effects, and their only daughter, Bernita, was born in the South Pacific.

After two years on the island of Raiatea, they were moved to the Cook Islands—the delayed replacements for the Pipers. In 1918, they

The Sterlings in retirement in Australia in the 1950s.

were called to pioneer the mission work in the Marquesas Islands, which is another archipelago colonized by France. In 1922–1923, they had their one and only furlough to the United States; they were never to see their American families again. On their return to the South Pacific in 1924, the Sterlings were sent back to the Society Islands, where they remained until 1938. For the twenty years after 1918, Maybelle and George endured repeated illnesses, but they also faced fierce opposition from colonial authorities and settlers. They had to suffer mental stresses, and while this was true for many church members, including ones in Adventist heartlands, it was more marked in the South Pacific because Adventism was utterly alien to the French settlers. Even the British colonial officials in other islands, whose attitudes might have ameliorated those of their French counterparts, were skeptical about Seventh-day Adventists. The insults heaped on the Sterlings left psychological scars—and the scar tissue on their psyches lasted. Twenty years later, Maybelle reminisced to a friend: "We were derided as dogs; the other whites called us no better than dogs." They were denied service in shops, snubbed, shunned, and literally spat on.[10]

In the face of this hostility, however, they persevered and won converts from among both the French settlers and the local populations. From 1938 to 1942, George and Maybelle taught at New Zealand Missionary College. After this, George worked in pastoral evangelism until 1945. The couple then served for five years in northern New South Wales, where they retired from their career of ministry in December 1950. Unlike the Appel, Longway, and Warren families, they never returned to the land of their birth. Going as missionaries was, in a sense, a life sentence, but it was one they embraced joyfully and successfully.

---

1. Marriage certificate, July 2, 1903, *Michigan, Marriage Records, 1867–1952* (Provo, UT: Ancestry.com, 2015), online database; "Death of Dr. A. C. Selmon," *Review and Herald* 108, no. 23 (June 4, 1931): 32; Arthur C. Selmon passport application, November 13, 1903, *U.S. Passport Applications, 1795–1925* (Provo, UT: Ancestry.com, 2015), online database; "Certificate of Death," *Michigan, Death Records, 1867–1950* (Provo, UT: Ancestry.com, 2015), online database.

2. Family and career details from Longway's appointee/interdivision employee file, GCA, Record Group 21, file no. 5842.

3. Duane S. Johnson to Ezra Longway, June 7, 1972; Roger W. Coon, "Ezra Leon Longway: Life Sketch," December 15, 1987, p. 4, Longway appointee/interdivision employee file.

4. Service record in Longway appointee/interdivision employee file.

5. Ruth Wheeler, *Light the Paper Lantern* (Mountain View, CA: Pacific Press®, 1967), 120; Roger W. Coon, "Pastor M. C. Warren," *Far Eastern Division Outlook*, March 1970, 4.

6. Wheeler, *Light the Paper Lantern*, 120, 121; Coon, "Pastor M. C. Warren." See General

Conference of Seventh-day Adventists, *Yearbook of the Seventh-day Adventist Denomination, 1949* (Washington, DC: Review and Herald®, 1949), 95; General Conference of Seventh-day Adventists, *Yearbook of the Seventh-day Adventist Denomination, 1950* (Washington, DC: Review and Herald®, 1950), 121; General Conference of Seventh-day Adventists, *Yearbook of the Seventh-day Adventist Denomination, 1951* (Washington, DC: Review and Herald®, 1951), 125; General Conference of Seventh-day Adventists, *Yearbook of the Seventh-day Adventist Denomination, 1952* (Washington, DC: Review and Herald®, 1952), 113; General Conference of Seventh-day Adventists, *Seventh-day Adventist Yearbook, 1953* (Washington, DC: Review and Herald®, 1953), 14, 116, 120.

7. Service record and correspondence in Appel appointee file, GCA, Record Group 21, file no. 47611; "Appel," Obituaries, *North Pacific Union Gleaner* 77, no. 8 (April 19, 1982): 23, 24.

8. Appel appointee file, file no. 47611. For Appel-Coulston correspondence, including a number of letters from Laura Appel to Leatha Coulston after Elmer's death, see Elmer F. Coulston Collection, Department of Archives and Special Collections, Loma Linda University.

9. Marye Trim, "Sterling, George Leighton and Maybelle Henrietta (Klopfenstein)," in "Encyclopedia of Seventh-day Adventists," ed. D. J. B. Trim, Dragoslava Santrac, et al. (forthcoming).

10. This was shared with the author's mother in the 1950s when the author's father was pastoring the church in which the Sterlings, who had retired, were members.

CHAPTER 11

"They Would Willingly Sacrifice Their Lives":
Inter-America and South America

Today, the Inter-American Division of the Seventh-day Adventist Church is the division with the largest number of church members. The South American Division is not far behind, especially because its membership is regularly audited and thus is credible (in contrast to membership numbers for some divisions on other continents). But how did the tropical regions of the Caribbean, Central America, and the northern half of South America become such strongholds of the Seventh-day Adventist faith? We saw earlier that it was partly because the delicate shoots of the Adventist faith, planted in tropical soil by missionaries, was watered by their blood. Seventh-day Adventism in the Inter-American Division was also nurtured by years and years of service by many, many missionaries. Again, a few examples of these missionaries must suffice.

The extent to which missionaries served for long periods in Inter-America is remarkable because the tropics of Central America were particularly arduous to serve in, especially during the early years of the twentieth century. If missionaries survived the region, however, they often spent many years there—and literally did not want to leave, even if their lives were in danger.

William Edgar Baxter Sr. and his wife, Verna, spent more than three decades as missionaries in Central America. Like so many missionaries, they volunteered to serve overseas in their twenties. Consequently, William studied at the Washington Foreign Mission Seminary in Takoma Park, Maryland, from 1906 to 1909. In early 1909, he was called to Jamaica, where the Baxters served in pastoral ministry in Kingston for two years.

In 1917, William and Verna, both thirty-five years old, were called back to the Caribbean. William had been the president of the Arkansas Conference for nearly four years. He was called to pastoral ministry in Venezuela, which was then part of the South Caribbean Conference. Some people would see this change as a demotion, and many church leaders would have continued along the easy path that led higher in the denominational hierarchy while enjoying the comforts of life in the United States. William and Verna, however, accepted the call to Venezuela. Two years later, William became the first director (president) of the newly founded Venezuela Mission. William and Verna served in the Inter-American Division for thirty-four years, only returning for good early in 1949, when William was well past the age of sixty-seven and Verna already sixty-eight.[1]

William had pastored in Jamaica and Venezuela; was the director of the Venezuela Mission (1919–1923); was the superintendent (president) of the Caribbean Union Mission (1923–1927) and the Central American Union Mission (1927–1935); was the director of the Upper Magdalena Mission (1937–1943); taught Bible classes at

the Colombia-Venezuela Union Training School (1943–1944); and was the president of the Panama Conference (1945–1946) and, again, the Upper Magdalena Mission (1947–1949). William and Verna had lived in Colombia, Costa Rica, Curaçao, Jamaica, Panama, and Venezuela; additionally, William had spent much time in the other European colonies of the eastern Caribbean and the northern coast of South America. In 1949, they returned "home" only because of poor health: a colleague wrote with concern of how William "has fainted a couple of times right in the street."[2]

William Baxter in 1922.

By 1949, the problem was not that Baxter was just starting to suffer sustained illnesses—it was that he was too old to resist their effects. Earlier, in 1935, his health had caused concern: suffering from anemia and tuberculosis, he was obliged to return to the United States for treatment only two years after his previous furlough.[3] A physician, reporting after a medical examination of William at Washington Sanitarium and Hospital, stated that Baxter was "suffering from a bit of nerve exhaustion due to climatic depletion, and also to heavy work, which most of these men experience in their interest in the work." While expressed in dated language, the statement makes plain the considerable physical and mental strain put on frontline workers in difficult mission fields—and their tendency to overwork, which was discussed in chapters 6 and 7. Similar words were written by a colleague of Baxter: William was "a sick, worn man."[4]

So committed was William to the work, however, that he always placed it above his own needs. In 1936, the Inter-American Division president, G. A. Roberts, wrote that Baxter "is a wonderful Christian. His wife's influence is excellent. They truly love the Lord and they love this third angel's message and would willingly sacrifice their lives for it."[5] William came close to doing just that but

Photo of William and Verna Baxter, taken for their passport renewal in 1949 when they finally returned to the United States. The toll of their years of strain and illness are clearly evident.

somehow survived: during his thirty-four years of service in Central America, he "was nearly drowned, and . . . ruptured his right lung"; broke bones on five occasions; came under the guns of revolutionaries; twice endured serious bouts of malaria; suffered the temporary loss of feeling and limited paralysis in his limbs; and was afflicted with whipworm. By the mid-1940s, he was suffering again from pernicious anemia, and by 1948, he experienced "marked irregularity in the heartbeat"—presumably what would be termed atrial fibrillation today.[6]

William Baxter was reluctant to leave the mission field. Years earlier, his return from his medical leave was delayed until 1937 because of the aftereffects of tuberculosis and pernicious anemia, which required months of treatment. He was so ill that officers of the General Conference had voted to place him on "sustentation" (the church's retirement pension). G. A. Roberts, adding to his statement that William and Verna "would willingly sacrifice their lives" for the third angel's message, wrote the following: "How much better it would be for them to remain in America." But Baxter objected strongly to this attempt to save his life! He appealed the decision and obtained a positive medical certification.[7]

Baxter volunteered to return not just to Central America but to serve in the Upper Magdalena Mission in Colombia. This was, as he wrote, "a very needy field and has never as yet been fully organized and manned, for no one has remained there long enough to do this." The post of director was indeed vacant. That this was a demotion in terms of the denomination's hierarchy did not deter him—as it did not deter Merritt Warren a few years later in the Far East. Baxter's selfless offer was accepted, and as we have seen, he spent several years leading the mission field, helping to grow its membership from around two hundred people to more than seven hundred.[8]

William and Verna's children both served as missionaries in the Inter-American Division. The older of the two, Elizabeth, had been born in Jamaica; as an adult, she taught at the Central American Academy in Costa Rica for nearly three years (1927–1929). The younger child, William E. "Bill" Baxter Jr., and his wife, Marian, went to Colombia in 1938, where he was a colporteur and evangelist until 1940. He served as a pastor and evangelist in Colombia and Venezuela from 1940 to 1945 and taught Bible classes at Adventist seminaries in Mexico from 1946 to 1954. After four years of pastoring in the States, Bill and Marian returned to Mexico, teaching Bible classes at Montemorelos from 1958 to 1963. Thirteen years later, Bill and Marian, who were sixty and fifty-nine respectively, returned to Mexico, with Bill working in aviation ministry until 1980. In all, they spent twenty-six years in service in Central America.[9]

Elizabeth Baxter.

Marian and William Baxter Jr. in 1939.

Many years earlier, William Baxter Sr. had helped to recruit two more self-sacrificial missionaries to Central America—Alfred W. and Elizabeth Cott.[10] The Cotts worked for nine years among "two tribes of Indians": the "Akawaio and Arekuna," who were located in the Mount Roraima region at the intersection of Guyana, Venezuela, and Brazil. Among Adventists, these tribes were often known as the "Davis" Indians, named after Ovid Davis, who was the first Protestant missionary to reach the region and who died among them in 1911. They were then cut off from Westerners until Baxter and C. B. Sutton found them; they located Davis's grave in 1925. After reconnecting with the Akawaio and Arekuna tribes, there was a need for new missionaries to work among these people, who lived literally off the map because cartographers had yet to delineate the Mount Roraima region.[11]

Alfred Cott was born in Britain in 1887 and studied at Cambridge

University, but he converted to Seventh-day Adventism in 1921, gave up his studies, and emigrated to the United States. He later qualified as a nurse at the Glendale Sanitarium in California. Elizabeth was born in Nebraska in 1894, but she, too, graduated from the nursing course at Glendale.[12] Their journey to the mission field took them from San Francisco through the Panama Canal and then "eight days on the boat to Trinidad, then across to Georgetown, British Guiana," and finally "400 miles interior to a place so remote and unentered that the last 150 miles . . . [had to] be made on foot with Indian guides and carriers."[13] This last part of the journey, through the mountains and jungle, took them five and a half weeks.[14]

This photograph of Alfred W. and Elizabeth Cott was taken for their wedding.

The Cotts were isolated, faced huge challenges, and had an overwhelming workload. Even a short journey required considerable physical effort—slogging through the jungle on foot or paddling a canoe on often dangerous mountain streams and rivers. And ministry at the mission station was all consuming.

In 1933, Elizabeth wrote how they had recently cut down a "purple heart tree," hollowed it out, tarred it, and painted it green and grey, and thus, they had a new canoe. Alfred was off traveling in it, leaving all the work of the mission station to her. She wrote about teaching vegetarian cooking and how "young girls and young wives are already making new dishes, but the older ones don't like the new food. They will soo[n] though I think." But she also wrote matter-of-factly: "I sure have been busy from 5:45 a.m. until 10:00 p.m., and after holding meetings with the Indians, teaching school, and looking after the sick and various other duties."[15]

It was a daily regimen that many missionaries of the early 1900s would have recognized. In some respects, however, the Cotts' burden was greater than that faced by most missionaries.

After their enforced return to the United States, due to chronic ill health, H. T. Elliott, an associate secretary of the General Conference, told a colleague: "These good people have carried on with their work under conditions that few, if any of our workers in the world have to face . . . , farther isolated by travel, perhaps, than almost any of our missionaries in the world." Despite the enormous difficulties in visiting the people for whom they were working, the Cotts had, nevertheless, "faithfully" undertaken "their evangelistic and medical work . . . until Sister Cott's health broke and it became apparent that they could not remain amidst these difficulties in tropical climate longer." They had, he concluded, "risked everything they have, and even their lives."[16]

Alfred, Elizabeth, and their daughter, Joyce, all started to suffer from malaria soon after their arrival and continued to do so throughout their time in Guyana, with Alfred's case becoming chronic. Furthermore, for Alfred and Elizabeth, malaria remained in their systems long term. But these were not their only afflictions. When the Cotts returned from the mission field in late February 1935, their medical tests showed that "they all had hookworm. . . . They also all had amoeba." Elizabeth was suffering badly from amoebic dysentery and malaria as well as other illnesses, including some that were probably as a result of intense nervous strain on top of the infection. By the summer of 1935, Alfred was free of hookworms and amoebic infection, but even after much treatment, Elizabeth and Joyce were still suffering from them. Elizabeth had undergone, in the judgment of a senior church leader, a complete "breakdown of health . . . because of the unstinted service that she gave." She required "three major operations" in a hospital when in the United States and also suffered from chronic diseases. For many months after they left Guyana, Elizabeth continued to have poor health. In September 1936, her husband observed that she was still not "free of amoeba and malaria," and physicians in California were perplexed as to the continued incidence of malaria attacks and of chronic "terrible headaches."[17]

Even ten years earlier, certainly twenty, there is little doubt that the Cotts would have perished; however, by the 1930s, they could be treated effectively once they returned from their remote outpost. But this did not mean that they did not suffer and continue to suffer once they had returned home. This, too, was a familiar story to many other missionaries of the period. And like other missionaries, their intense labor and pains were not without fruit. During the eight years that the Cotts had served among the Akawaio and Arekuna tribes, they had established two local churches with 116 members in Guyana and had won other converts on the Venezuelan side of the ill-defined border.

Further to the south, the Amazon rain forest and the Andes Mountains posed different but difficult challenges. Among those who took them on were Dick and Jo Hayden.

Richard Augustus Hayden was born on May 31, 1903, in Los Angeles, California, but he grew up in Eugene, Oregon. In Eugene, the possibility of a career as a professional football player opened up for the strapping six-foot young man; to this end, he attended the University of Oregon for a year. But then, influenced by his older sister Lottie, he transferred to Walla Walla College. During Dick's last year of college, W. I. Smith, the president of Walla Walla College, ended the Week of Prayer with a call for students to embrace missionary service. Dick Hayden told a friend, "I have been led here for a definite purpose." Some years earlier, he had heard Floyd Bresee, a missionary to Peru, speak at a Young People's Missionary Volunteer meeting and had been inspired. Dick decided that "if God is willing, I will go to South America when I finish my college training."

He graduated in 1927 with a bachelor's degree in education and taught in a church school in the Columbia Valley. He felt a calling to the ministry and began evangelistic work in 1929 in Washington, but he still felt impressed to work in South America. Dick and his new wife, Georgiana "Jo," accepted an invitation to missionary service in the Inca Union Mission of the South American Division. They sailed for Peru in September 1930. Richard was twenty-seven, and Georgiana was twenty-one.

For their first three years, Dick served as a local pastor in the Amazon Mission, working under the inspirational leadership of legendary missionaries Ferdinand and Ana Stahl. Dick and Jo were based in Iquitos—a remote village, deep in Peru's Amazonian region. Their first child, Richard Dean, was born there in 1932. In 1933, the Haydens moved eight hundred miles south to the Andes Mountains to serve in the Lake Titicaca Training School in Juliaca, where Dick was the principal. After sixteen months, he was appointed as the secretary (director) of the Young People's Missionary Volunteer, Field Missionary, and Education Departments of the Lake Titicaca Mission, which was headquartered in Puno. Dick and Jo's second son was born in Arequipa in 1935. A third child, Carolyn, was born in Spokane, Washington, while they were on furlough in 1936, but all three were raised in South America.[18]

In some ways, the Andes have a better climate than the jungles of the Amazon and are less deadly in terms of disease. But there is still the risk of altitude sickness, and its early symptoms can be highly unpleasant, which, if not treated, can be fatal. However, when the Haydens lived in Peru, a range of tropical "fevers" and other little-known diseases were endemic in the mountains. Although medical science by the 1930s had advanced considerably from where it had been before World War I, there were still limited options for up-to-date medical care in the Andes, as in the upper Amazon, partly because both areas were remote. In addition, the Andes were characterized by poverty and deliberate neglect on the part of the authorities and landowners, who were eager to maintain their wealth at the expense of the local peoples.

The Hayden family in 1936.

(This social and economic oppression was something Adventist missionaries, such as Ferdinand Stahl and Dick Hayden, combated; they encouraged the Andean and Amazonian tribes to resist, albeit peacefully.) All this meant that it was still dangerous to serve as a missionary in the Andes in the 1930s. If the adults were less likely to perish than twenty or twenty-five years before, their children were all too often at risk, not just of illness but of death. A potent reminder of this fact was an Adventist graveyard, high in the Andes, in which several missionaries' children were buried (photograph on p. 122).[19]

While the threat of death could have been a powerful deterrent for missionaries such as Dick and Jo Hayden, who had three young children, they did not seem to have taken it into account, trusting God to work in their lives as He saw fit. In 1937, the family left Peru, as Dick had been called to the Bolivia Mission as Sabbath School, Education, and Young People's Missionary Volunteer secretary. After three years' service in Bolivia, he was elected director (president) of the Upper Amazon Mission, and he served there for eight years. In 1948–1949, he briefly worked in education again as a Bible professor at Inca Union College in Lima—Peru's capital and largest city. But then in 1949, he was called to the Inca Union Mission headquarters, also in Lima, as Home Missionary and Sabbath School secretary. He served in that capacity until 1959, when Dick and Jo moved to Ecuador, where Dick had been elected president of the Ecuador Mission. But

A Seventh-day Adventist graveyard high in the mountains of Bolivia, where a cluster of deceased missionary children, sometimes the only children of their parents, were buried in lonely graves.

after not quite two years, it was back to Peru, where Dick became the first president of the new North Peru Mission. He served in that capacity from 1961 through 1963, before stepping down to allow another leader to serve as president. For the Haydens' last four and a half years in Peru, Dick stayed in the North Peru Mission, serving as the secretary of the Lay Activities, Sabbath School, and Radio and Television Departments.

Dick and Jo left Peru for the United States, which they may no longer have thought of as home, in July 1968. Earlier, in August 1967, their son Richard Dean, who was thirty-five and had spent his career teaching in Adventist academies on the West Coast, had accepted a call to mission service in the Inter-American Division. He served in Puerto Rico for ten months but found this too much like the United States, and he was able to arrange a transfer to the Nicaragua Mission, where he served for a little more than two years. Sadly, in November 1970, while on his first furlough, he died in a plane crash near Pacific Union College. Richard Dean Hayden was thirty-eight.[20] Richard Augustus Hayden died on September 24, 1990, at the age of eighty-seven; Georgiana died on Christmas Eve 1996, also at the age of eighty-seven.

Dick and Jo Hayden had served as missionaries in Peru, Bolivia, and Ecuador for thirty-seven years and nine months. Except for eleven years at the Inca Union Mission and its college, they had worked at the local level: they spent twenty-six years in frontline mission work.

Dick Hayden was never a union officer and never held a position at the division headquarters. In the eyes of some, his career would be counted as mediocre and undistinguished. In Christ's eyes, however, the Haydens surely were seen as heroic. Their spirit comes out in a letter Dick wrote to the General Conference on April 30, 1968, confirming their retirement. He wrote, "Mrs. Hayden and I have been laboring here in the Inca Union since 1930, and it is hard for us to leave our many friends here. We are glad however to see these younger Peruvian men take over." His career was marked not by pride nor a craving for promotion in the denomination's hierarchy but by a passion to push the work forward and to reach the day when the local leaders were able to take over so that missionaries could stand aside, as Dick did in the North Peru Mission. But the missionaries' sacrifice and commitment in the early days laid the foundation for the twenty-first-century church in Latin America.

In 1930, when Dick and Jo arrived in Peru, there were 7,450 church members in the Inca Union Mission, encompassing Peru, Ecuador, and Bolivia. When they left in 1968, the Inca Union's membership was 54,548, or growth by a factor of 7. As of June 30, 2018, those three nations were organized in four unions that had a total audited membership of 576,076: this area has grown by a factor of 77 since 1930. The exponential growth came when the Peruvians, Bolivians, and Ecuadorians took the place of the missionaries. But it was the missionaries who had laid the foundations in the 1930s, '40s, '50s, and '60s.

William Baxter Sr. and his family—Verna, Elizabeth, and William Jr.; Alfred and Elizabeth Cott; Richard Augustus, Georgiana, and Richard Dean Hayden: they stand for the many missionaries whose labors bore rich fruit in today's huge membership in South America and Inter-America. Between them, the Baxters and the Haydens served 175 years in Inter-America and South America.

1. W. E. and Mrs. W. E. Baxter, "Biographical Information Blanks," 1917–1945, in GCA, Record Group 21, "Personal Information Forms and Biographical Material—1950," Box "B to Bea"; "Information on Returning Missionaries" forms, March 16, 1949; and Baxter appointee file, Record Group 21, file no. 45206. See also "Fruitful Service in God's Cause," *Inter-American Division Messenger* 26, no. 5 (May 1949): 7.

2. W. E. Murray to N. W. Dunn, Baxter appointee file, GCA Record Group 21, file no. 45206.

3. General Conference officers meeting, October 16, 1935, GCA, Record Group 2, vol. II, p. 1476.

4. Dr. C. S. Parrett to A. W. Cormack, July 30, 1935; A. R. Ogden to H. T. Elliott, April 2, 1937, General Conference Officer's minutes, GCA, Record Group 21, appointee file 45206.

5. G. A. Roberts to H. T. Elliott, December 30, 1936, GCA, Record Group 21, appointee file 45206.

6. Medical reports and correspondence, Baxter appointee file, GCA, Record Group 21, file no. 45206; George C. Nickle, "Successful Recovery," *Inter-American Division Messenger* 25, no. 6 (August 1948): 2.

7. General Conference officers meeting, October 16, 1935, November 17, 1935, August 19, 1936, and December 20, 1936, GCA, General Conference Officers' Minutes, Record Group 2, vol. II, pp. 1476, 1546, 1945, 2094; G. A. Roberts to H. T. Elliott, n. 5; General Conference Secretariat memoranda and correspondence, November 1935–February 1937, GCA, Record Group 21, appointee file 45206.

8. See General Conference of Seventh-day Adventists, *Year Book of the Seventh-day Adventist Denomination, 1937* (Washington, DC: Review and Herald*, 1937), 145, 146; W. E. Baxter to H. T. Elliott, April 4, 1937, GCA, Record Group 21, appointee file 45206. General Conference of Seventh-day Adventists, *Year Book of the Seventh-day Adventist Denomination, 1938* (Washington, DC: Review and Herald*, 1938), 149, 150; General Conference of Seventh-day Adventists, *Year Book of the Seventh-day Adventist Denomination, 1943* (Washington, DC: Review and Herald*, 1943), 126.

9. E. G. Baxter, "Biographical Information Blanks," 1937; W. E. Baxter Jr. and Marian Baxter, "Biographical Information Blanks," 1939–1963; Mr. and Mrs. W. E. Baxter Jr., "Personal Information Forms," 1976, in GCA, Record Group 21, "Personal Information Forms and Biographical Material—1950," Box "B to Bea;" W. E. Baxter Jr. appointee/interdivision employee file, GCA, Record Group 21, file no. 7948.

10. A. W. Cott to B. E. Beddoe, February 1, 1926; E. G. Baxter to E. E. Andross, August 10, 1926, GCA, Record Group 21, appointee files 45206 and 45512.

11. M. E. Kern, "Conversation With A. W. Cott," March 20, 1935, Cott appointee file, GCA, Record Group 21, file no. 45512. Baxter describes his rediscovery of the Davis Indians in a long report to E. E. Andross, November 23, 1925, Baxter appointee file, GCA, Record Group 21, file no. 45206. Elizabeth Cott later published two books about the Davis Indians: Elizabeth Buhler Cott, *Trailing the Davis Indians* (Mountain View, CA: Pacific Press*, 1936); Elizabeth Buhler Cott, *Jewels From Green Hell: Stories of the Davis Indians of British Guiana* (Washington, DC: Review and Herald*, 1969).

12. Alfred W. Cott and Mrs. A. W. Cott, "General Conference Questionnaire[s]," October 30, 1924, GCA, Record Group 21, appointee file 45512.

13. J. R. Ferren, "At the Cross Roads," *Pacific Union Recorder* 26, no. 13 (November 4, 1926): 1. Ferren was a missionary in Panama.

14. See ibid.; H. T. Elliott to Glenn Calkins, March 10, 1935, Cott appointee file, GCA, Record Group 21, file no. 45512.

15. Mrs. A. W. Cott to W. H. Elliott, May 23, 1933, Cott, appointee file 45512.

16. Elliott to Calkins (n14); W. H. Elliott to E. K. Slade, March 10, 1935, Cott, appointee file 45512.

17. General Conference Secretariat memoranda, medical reports, and correspondence from and about the Cotts, in Cott appointee file 45512.

18. Richard A. Hayden and Gwendolen Lampshire Hayden, *From Football Field to Mission Field* (Washington, DC: Review and Herald®, 1951); Richard A. Hayden appointee file, GCA, Record Group 21, file no. 48285; and the *SDA Yearbook*, annual editions.

19. M. E. Kern, "Urgent Calls for Missionary Doctors," *Review and Herald* 107, no. 51 (October 2, 1930): 32.

20. Richard Dean Hayden appointee file, GCA, Record Group 21, file no. 16743. See also the book by Richard D. Hayden's widow, Iris Hayden Stober, *God Leads in Perplexities, Joys, and Sorrows* (Fort Oglethorpe, GA: TEACH Services, 2013).

CHAPTER 12

A Living Sacrifice in Spite of Death

Some of the most heroic and selfless examples of long-term mission service are of those men and women who lost a spouse or a child and yet continued or later resumed their foreign mission service. Sometimes these missionaries even served in the places where they had buried a loved one—or loved *ones*. The few examples that follow could be multiplied many times, but the self-sacrifice of the Konigmacher family is particularly marked.

In 1908, Samuel M. Konigmacher mailed a truly tragic postcard to T. E. Bowen in the General Conference Secretariat. In April 1908, Samuel, who was thirty, and his twenty-eight-year-old wife, Ruth, had sailed from New York City. They arrived at the Malamulo Mission station in British Central Africa (present-day Malawi) on July 15 but soon after moved to Matandani, which was a remote "out-station" of Malamulo.[1] Their first child, Samuel Martin Jr., was born in October. On December 18, Samuel Sr. recorded his son's passing, writing to Bowen on a postcard that bears an image of his home state of Pennsylvania:

Dear Bro[ther],
Our little boy died last night with fever and an acute attack of indigestion. We buried him today. We will miss him much.
Respectfully.
S. Konigmacher

The note is concise, with little emotion expressed, but the distress is unmistakable. The General Conference executive committee voted to send "an expression of sympathy," which was doubtless appreciated for the sentiment, but it could have done little to ease the heartache.[2]

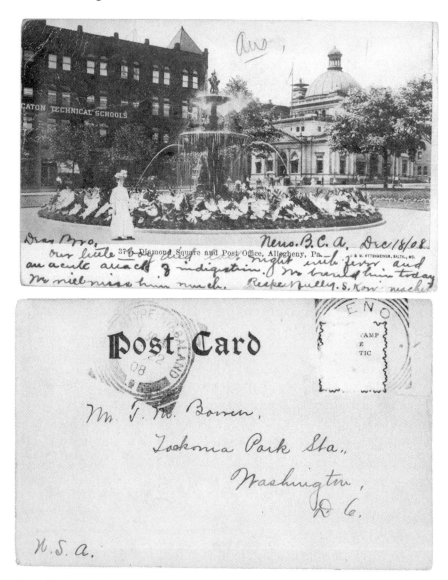

Samuel Konigmacher's postcard

Sadly, little Samuel was not the last son the Konigmachers lost during their time in Africa. Three more boys—Arthur, James, and Joseph—were born in the mission field, and two were buried there: James in 1914, and Joseph in 1917.

Yet the Konigmacher family continued serving selflessly in Africa. Samuel and Ruth had their only furloughs in 1913 (when Samuel was a General Conference session delegate) and 1924. They spent their lives pioneering the work in remote and difficult locations, pushing the boundaries of mission forward. In 1934, while serving in Barotseland (a part of present-day Zambia), Ruth fell ill; she was taken to Cape Town, South Africa, for treatment and died there on September 29. On hearing the news, H. T. Elliott, a senior church leader, wrote of Samuel and Ruth: "Their willingness to go and live under difficult conditions has been an inspiration to many of our missionaries." After Ruth's funeral, Samuel worked another six years before retiring, his health—and perhaps even his mental equilibrium—broken. He had served for thirty-two years as a missionary, burying four of his family in African soil.[3]

Baptism on the upper reaches of the Zambezi River

Samuel was a straightforward, plainspoken man; this was perhaps one reason why he loved working on the frontier, away from the sophistication of civilization, which he would later find perplexing during retirement. Yet in North America and South Africa, he was a popular speaker, telling stories from the mission field in a simple, sincere style and urging personal commitment to Adventist missions. His uncomplicated character and plain style may also have helped him to be successful in his work with Africans. An example of his missional success is seen in a remarkable photograph. It shows a baptism on the upper reaches of the Zambezi River, with boats arranged to block off the approach of crocodiles, so that the new church members could be baptized in safety. How many baptismal candidates have willingly dared crocodile attack! But this photo is also believed to portray Samuel Konigmacher. It comes from a folder of photos brought home by E. D. Dick after touring Africa in 1924; he described the scene as the "first baptism" at Kalembezi Mission, which Konigmacher had helped to establish and where he had conducted the first baptisms in 1921 or 1922.[4]

The Konigmachers were criticized by other missionaries in the 1920s for being too close to the local people. In the winter of 1934, a white church leader in South Africa wrote sneeringly that Samuel could not be placed "in charge of European work. . . . His whole life . . . has been given to the work of the primitive native tribes." This attempt at reproach was expressed in terms we would not use today, but now it seems like praise. H. T. Elliott wrote using similar language but meant it positively: "He wanted to get out among the raw heathen." Samuel himself contentedly reminisced about sharing stories with local people in their language while "visiting with them around their camp fires." After his death, Ruth's sister said simply: "His heart was in Africa."[5]

The Konigmachers were remarkable for the number of family members who died, but they were not unique in their willingness to remain in service. As we saw in part 1, David Babcock buried two wives—one in the Caribbean—and went into the mission field with a third wife. Yet he continued as a missionary, providing strong leadership to the nascent mission in West Africa and later returning to the West Indies where one wife was buried. His third wife, Mina, accompanied David and his children throughout the rest of his mission service.

Studio portrait of David and Mina Babcock and his children, taken c. 1919.

Earlier we saw that Gentry G. Lowry remained in Southern Asia when he could have retired to Tennessee and been honored for his achievements in missional leadership. But was it really his home at that point? Truly, had he and Bertha "called to mind that country from which they had come out, they would have had opportunity to return. But . . . they desire[d] a better, that is, a heavenly country" (Hebrews 11:15, 16). And they were committed to the peoples of India.

This remained true for Gentry Lowry's family following his death. Bertha had been twenty-three when she went to India; at the time of Gentry's death in 1942, she was fifty-six. She did go "home": she served thirteen more years in India, returning to the United States only in 1955 at the age of sixty-nine. She spent forty-six years of her life as a missionary to India and Burma; Gentry was a missionary for thirty-three years. Their sons, Willis and Roscoe, were raised in India, where Roscoe was born. Both returned to India as missionaries themselves: Roscoe served for forty-two years, from 1941 to 1983, including thirteen years as the Southern Asia Division president, while Willis served for thirty-four years, from 1947 to 1981. Between them, the family dedicated 155 years to the Southern Asia Division. Such was the love the family had for India and Indian Adventists. Such was the passion they had for reaching India with the good news and prophetic truth.[6]

In chapter 4, we saw that Charles Sutton tragically lost his wife, Dottie, the day after they arrived as missionaries in Trinidad. The expatriate community in Port of Spain expected the widower to return to the United States with his daughter and were astonished when they stayed. As Charles wrote to his sister Sadie, "God called me to Trinidad. . . . I am going to stay."[7] Charles and Eleanor did stay, and both spent much of the rest of their lives in mission service. In 1920, two years after being widowed, Charles remarried. His second wife was Christine DeSilva, who was a Trinidadian. Their

Willis and Roscoe Gentry, photographed in India with their parents in 1919.

marriage lasted forty-four years, and they were missionaries for thirty years in Trinidad and Tobago, Venezuela, Guyana, Belize, and Panama.

In spite of the loss of her mother when she was only seven years old, Eleanor did not become hostile to mission service. She married a physician, Willis G. Dick, and they went as missionaries to the Far East in 1947; they served together for twenty-nine years in China, Malaysia, and the Philippines. In 1965, their youngest child, Lora, was killed in a car accident while studying in France. "Our hearts are broken, but our faith is strong," they wrote to friends. "Please pray for us [and the] many souls for whom we labor. Pray that this victory for Satan may be turned in some way we know not—to a great victory for God."[8] For grieving parents who might have blamed God, these were noble sentiments, but they are also strikingly similar to those expressed by surviving spouses and parents six and seven decades before.

While these missionaries' grief was heartfelt, most saw beyond the missing faces and looked past what they had lost, even as they mourned. They had more than the blessed hope of the resurrection; they had the ongoing, urgent task of proclaiming the gospel and prophetic truth. This sense of purpose diminished death's sting; vigorously preaching Christ's victory over the grave hastened the day of its final defeat; and their redoubling efforts renewed their hope.

---

1. See S. M. and Mrs. S. M. Konigmacher, "Biographical Information Blank[s]," July 12, 1912, Konigmacher appointee file, GCA, Record Group 21, file no. 46243; S. M. Konigmacher, "East Central Africa," *Life and Health* 24, no. 4 (April 1909): 237, 238; S. M. Konigmacher, "Nyassaland, Africa," *Review and Herald* 86, no. 20 (May 20, 1909): 19; J. V. Willson, "South African Union Conference: Review of the Mission Field," *Review and Herald* 86, no. 22 (June 3, 1909): 20.

2. General Conference Executive Committee meeting of Feb. 8, 1909, GCA, Proceedings, vol. VII, p. 592; news note, *Review and Herald* 86, no. 7 (February 18, 1909): 24.

3. Cable to General Conference, October 2, 1934; H. T. Elliott to Paul C. Mason and to Mrs. A. E. Hall, October 4, 1934; S. M. Konigmacher to "Brethren" of General Conference Committee, October 5, 1934; S. M. Konigmacher to W. H. Branson and African Division Committee, March 2, 1924, Konigmacher appointee file, GCA, Record Group 21, file no. 46243.

4. W. H. Branson, "Africa," *Field Tidings* 13, no. 32 (September 21, 1921): 5; E. D. Dick, "Kalembezi and Rusangu Camp-Meeting," *African Division Outlook* 22, no. 18 (September 15, 1924): 4.

5. A. E. Nelson to J. L. Shaw and M. E. Kern, June 29, 1934; H. T. Elliott to Paul C. Mason, October 4, 1934, Konigmacher appointee file, GCA, Record Group 21, file no. 46243.

6. Service record details from appointee/interdivision employee files, GCA, Record Group 21, G. G. and Bertha Lowry, file no. 48621; Roscoe S. Lowry, file no. 4681; Willis G. Lowry, file no. 7208.

7. Arthur E. Sutton, "Sutton," Necrology, *Inter-American Messenger* 41, no. 9 (September 1964): 12.

8. "Dr. and Mrs. W. G. Dick" to Elder Sorensen, June 11, 1965, W. G. Dick appointee file, GCA, Record Group 21, file no. 13439.

"How Can We Let Them Know?"

Whathat can I say about the many stories that have been told in this book—stories of selflessness, sadness, tragedy, and trial, yet also of triumph? I think of each story, each life of service to others, and each grave of mission-minded men, women, and children as links in a chain. The great chain of mission circles the globe and binds Seventh-day Adventists together. It was forged in suffering, sacrifice, and zeal but also in love—love for fellow human beings who would perish eternally without knowing Jesus.

Some may believe this thought to be a trifle fanciful, yet I am not the first person to think of the analogy of a chain when considering missionary sacrifice. George F. Enoch wrote the following after the death of his brother Charles in Trinidad: "We have no regrets to offer, but take this bereavement as one more link to bind our lives on the altar of missionary endeavor."[1]

For Enoch, a missionary's death helped to forge a chain that linked missionaries to service; for who could disregard such a sacrifice? But an alternative view of a chain of "missionary endeavor" is that each link, each life of service, inspires another life of service until the message of Revelation 14 spans the globe. This was the perspective of William Spicer—a missionary to two continents who nursed Dores A. Robinson on his deathbed—before he became an officer of the General Conference. Spicer wrote in 1906 of "the inspiration of lives true and loyal unto the death. It is one field and one service—the third angel's message to all the world."[2]

In Enoch's letter, we have the language of a living sacrifice: his brother's life had been offered "on the altar of missionary endeavor." This dedication in the face of difficulty and tragedy raises the inevitable question: What drove these men and women to offer up their lives as living sacrifices? Their motivation must have been none other than their passion for sharing the good news and saving souls. And it is with this passion for the gospel proclamation, for disciple making, and for the salvation of men and women that we will end.

In 1899, Frederick W. Brown, who, as we saw earlier, died of smallpox later that year in India, wrote from London where he and his wife, Katie, would board a ship for Calcutta. Describing how he and Katie had felt as they left the Battle Creek, Michigan, train station en route to New York and the beginning of their voyage to India, he wrote, "As the train sped on its way, there was joy in our hearts . . . because we were taking the message of the third angel to that ancient land."[3] Later, writing from Ranchi, not long before he passed away, he fervently expressed his hope that "God grant that many may see the truth, and repent before it is too late."[4]

In 1902, after Albert Fischer died of typhoid fever in Puerto Rico, his colleague A. J. Haysmer reported on his last days: "During this time he often spoke of the work which he had only begun; and knowing his condition, he plead [sic] with me not to neglect the work in this island, for he believed that there were many precious souls here. He seemed to worry, thinking that perhaps his death would keep others from coming to this field; but I assured him that this would affect only the faint hearted; that the true soldiers would be stimulated to press to the front, and fill the ranks, perhaps two or three taking the place of one."[5]

Some missionaries went overseas without the enthusiasm of Brown and Fischer. Living, however, among those who needed to "see the truth" kindled in them that same passion for saving "precious souls." For example, in 1896, Dr. Joseph Caldwell wrote from the Cook Islands to friends in the United States how, months earlier, when he "was called . . . to go abroad," he had been enjoying the medical work in the American South and accepted the call a little reluctantly. "I thought I should never have so much interest in another field," he wrote, "but I now . . . have such a burden for these precious souls for whom I am now beginning to be able to labor spiritually, that I can indulge no vain regrets as to my field. I would not change, from choice, if I could."[6] As we have seen, when he and his wife, Julia, left Rarotonga, it was not by choice but because of her fatal illness.

In 1906, the *Review and Herald* published an article by Arthur Selmon, written from his mission station in Siang Cheng, to encourage missionary service. In it, he states the following:

> There is a great work yet to be done before . . . [the Second Coming] can take place; for this gospel of the kingdom shall be preached in all the world for a witness unto all the nations; and then shall the end come. . . .
>
> . . . Here we have three fourths of China's four hundred and twenty-six millions, and only nine workers to preach the message. . . .
>
> . . . We long to see reinforcements coming out to help us. You know this blessed truth, and what other call do you want to lead you out into the regions beyond?[7]

It is fascinating that Selmon uses the expression "the regions beyond" here as it was favored by Ellen White when calling for missions to world religions and the great unreached areas of the world. It shows how her ideas were spreading and shaping missionary activity, but it also shows the urgency, felt by missionaries to East Asia and Southern Asia in particular, of proclaiming the gospel of the kingdom not just to other Christians but to adherents of Islam, Hinduism, Confucianism, Daoism, and Buddhism.[8]

Selmon continues with two interesting ideas: First, he writes about what our commitment to cross-cultural mission—mission to those who are not Christians and, thus, are furthest away from understanding Christ—says about our faith in general. Second, he makes the argument that concentrating on a witness to those who have never heard of Christ may help us to deal with the challenges arising from materialism and secularism. Each argument is worth considering in the twenty-first century.

> The missionary activity of Seventh-day Adventists is the best index of their faith in the soon coming of the Lord. Those who feel and know that he is soon coming, will be using every energy to proclaim the gospel message to those who are yet in darkness. If all the young men and women in our training-schools had this conviction, what an incentive it would be to their work! They would be in no danger of becoming engrossed in any of the false sciences and speculative

philosophies that side-track some of our young people. . . .

So, my brother or sister, as you are surrounded by all the comforts of home life, and are planning to settle down in some enterprise simply for the sake of making a comfortable living, will you not think of China's millions that are perishing for a knowledge of the truth which makes your heart glad?[9]

Selmon's words are similar to those of Edwin and Lucy Webster when reporting about Trinidad in the pages of the *Review and Herald* ten years before:

By careful economy and self-denial on the part of all the workers, we have got along . . . so that most of the time we have what we need. We delight in the work of the Lord, and think not so much of our own little wants; but we trust that our brethren in America . . . will not allow the Lord's cause to suffer. Our brethren here are doing nobly toward supporting our work; but I know of many a brother in America who could do more than all these together.[10]

The pleas of Arthur Selmon and the Websters still resound today. They are a call to a renewal of the spirit of sacrifice. That is easy to say but far harder to do. I cannot but be humbled, however, as I consider the many men and women in their early twenties, even in their teens, who were willing to go far away and give their lives for others. May their examples inspire us.

Furthermore, the comments of Arthur Selmon and the Websters still apply to a great extent when it comes to financial support. Even though many parts of the world where missionaries worked are now self-supporting, others are decidedly not. If Seventh-day Adventists are to reach the world, then those with the greatest resources must help those with the least.

The Websters and Arthur Selmon each make another point, however, and this argument will bring us to the end of this book about sacrifice. They sound an alarm against complacency and ring a bell calling church members to urgency. Their point is that someone must go to those who do not know Jesus and tell these people about Him and His death for us. Selmon asks his American readers, "If your next-door neighbor" did not know the truth and were the victim of super-stition, "would you not do all in your power to point out the true God to him? The fact that China is a few thousand miles from you does not lessen your responsibility; for if you do not go, who will?"[11]

Edwin Webster writes similarly nine years earlier; reporting from the perspective of the Trinidadian, he declares: "We need your prayers, dear readers; and also devoted brethren to locate here to give a help-ing hand. Who will come?"[12]

––––––––––

We began with Eva May Clements. We will conclude with her and with her last known letter. It is a powerful testimony and all the more powerful because Eva Clements did not know that this would be her last letter. She may have written letters later, but none survive. Because she did not write it on her deathbed but while traveling on a journey that she had no inkling would be her last, without an eye to the future, there is no suggestion of calculation or artifice—of a desire to conform to Adventist ideas of a "good death" in which the writer might be expected to include an invocation to further service.

Instead, it just records what Eva thought. And it, therefore, shows how deep the commitment to worldwide mission was in early twentieth-century Adventism. Eva was not an evangelist nor even a major church leader; she was a stenographer—a secretary. But her com-mitment to the mission of the Seventh-day Adventist Church was complete.

In Calcutta, en route to Rangoon, she visited a temple and saw Hindu pilgrims worshiping an image of the goddess Kali. This memory stayed with Eva. In a letter to friends, she describes how "the people are standing about seven or eight feet deep before this huge monster, and the guide cannot make himself heard for the shouting and shuf-fling in the endeavour to worship the cruel deception of the enemy." But her mind was not focused on the image but the Indian people. She continues, "No privation, no sacrifice is too great for them to make to behold their god, many having come long distances for this purpose." And then her mind turned to how they might come to know Jesus:

"I pray for deeper consecration on the part of myself and others here, and for an inflow of workers from the homeland to this needy field. There is a great need and so much to do. You who are young and can learn the language are the ones who are most wanted. You who hate the works of darkness, and will with the aid of the lamp divine let His rays penetrate the gloom. Picture these poor people for whom Christ died. How can we let them know?"[13]

Eva's final words are powerful—especially because they are not the studied rhetoric of a church leader or public evangelist. They are the strongly held personal sentiments of a secretary. And they describe a need that is still urgent: "Picture these poor people for whom Christ died. How can we let them know?"

Despite the extraordinary global growth of the Seventh-day Adventist Church, growth that was built on living sacrifices, there are still billions of people "for whom Christ died" who know nothing of His sacrifice, resurrection, and heavenly ministry. A favorite early Adventist hymn was "Seeking the Lost". The lost are found everywhere, yet they are to be found more particularly in some places than in others.

Europe, "Christendom" in ages past, is post-Christian today; Australia and Canada are following fast down the same path. The United States is secularizing at speed, swayed by postmodernism and materialism—so, too, are Brazil, South Africa, and South Korea. These were the old, and are some of the new, chief recruiting grounds for Adventist missionaries.

God is calling people to minister in these contexts, finding innovative, creative, yet faithful ways to promote belief in the midst of radical disbelief. And missionaries from former European colonies, called to Western countries, have a part to play in this work. Yet, in spite of the new challenges faced in old Christian strongholds, the reality is that the Seventh-day Adventist Church in most of these affluent countries has the financial resources to evangelize its own territories and those engaged in that work of outreach face few real dangers.

The situation is very different across large parts of the globe, including the regions where the world's population is growing fastest. Today, there are many Seventh-day Adventist believers in China and in India, where so many missionaries died. Yet the Advent movement still has to reach, in large part, the people of China and India—and those in the Middle East, Southeast Asia, North Africa, and West Africa. This area is often called the 10/40 Window; this term, coined by a Christian missiologist, refers more or less to the latitudes between 10 and 40 degrees north of the equator. The lack of Adventist success in this vast area, which is home to two-thirds of the world's population, can hardly be ignored—no matter how fast the church grows in Latin America and sub-Saharan Africa.

Mission in the 10/40 Window is very difficult for many reasons. Medical care and public hygiene are often limited, and poverty, conflict, and corruption are widespread. Authoritarian regimes are common. The homelands of the great world religions are here, and there is deep-seated hostility from officials and often from ordinary people to Christian proselytism. In many places, to witness is to risk being beaten, imprisoned, tortured, or executed. In areas where mission stations exist, they are often remote and in unhealthy regions, which is why permission has been granted to open them. Church workers are in danger of serious illness, even death, from various diseases, including two that will be familiar from earlier in this book: malaria and blackwater fever. Across most of the 10/40 Window's huge territory, the Seventh-day Adventist Church has very limited internal resources and faces major external constraints.

In other words, the task that Adventist missionaries faced a hundred years ago, when Eva May Clements went to India and Myanmar, is still unfinished. Across the 10/40 Window, there is still the need for cross-cultural missionaries. Today, these missionaries may come from former mission fields—from places marked by missionary graves. Adventist missionaries come from anywhere and go everywhere. But the capacity to support missionaries and to provide much-needed resources to the 10/40 Window is not the same in all places.

In the technologically advanced and prosperous societies of North America, Europe, Australasia, and parts of South America, the church frequently is financially strong, certainly in relative terms. It is rich, too, in people: educated, skilled, healthy, and comparatively affluent church members from countries whose governments are likely to make some effort to help them if they fall ill, are injured, or imprisoned in foreign countries. Not all church members can go as missionaries, of course. Age, health, and family circumstances will shape how and where members serve, as will the different spiritual gifts bestowed by the Holy Spirit. And God calls some people to work in their local communities. But the commitment to mission and sacrifice can take many forms: those who cannot *go* can still *give* and *pray*. Church members in Western countries are especially well placed to sacrifice, whether by financially supporting cross-cultural missionaries or by serving in person, utilizing their valuable skill sets.

A particular responsibility for reaching the world remains with the original mission heartlands. Eva Clements, in her prayer "for an inflow of workers from the homeland to this needy field," identified both a continuing need and an enduring obligation.

From this survey of historical missionaries who gave their all, three questions stand out and still challenge Seventh-day Adventists today—the questions of Webster, Selmon, and Clements:

1. "Who will come?"
2. "If you do not go, who will?"
3. "How can we let them know" that Christ died for them?

But of all these questions, it is the third—Eva's question—that I find most compelling because she was not a pastor, medical missionary, or missionary leader. We might expect Pastor Webster and Dr. Selmon to pose these questions. Eva was, as many would see it, merely an administrative assistant. But her heart for mission was as strong, and her zeal for sharing Jesus was as burning as anyone's. And that I find inspiring.

And so, Eva's question is before us. The answer is that, in the church's present just as in its past, Seventh-day Adventists need to serve and sacrifice for frontline mission.

If we are going to "let them know," it requires money, generously given by members around the world, and prayers, fervently offered by members uniting around the world; it will certainly take skillful use of technology and media. Yet all that will not be enough. It will need some of us, now as in the past, to go to foreign countries and embrace their people as our own. It will require Seventh-day Adventists to reconnect with—to reclaim—the desire to share Jesus that motivated men and women of all ages to work as missionaries in other lands and other cultures, six, seven, ten, twelve decades ago.

We need to embrace anew the spirit of those men and women. Their spirit is what the church needs now: the spirit that says, whatever my age or circumstances, I will take responsibility for sharing Jesus with those who have never heard of Him. I will go. I will "let them know."

Seventh-day Adventists must again be willing to offer our bodies as living sacrifices.

---

1. George F. Enoch, quoted in W. A. S[picer], "Two Vacant Places in the Mission Field Ranks," *Review and Herald* 84, no. 9 (February 28, 1907): 5.

2. W. A. S[picer], "The Price of Victory," *Review and Herald* 83, no. 3 (January 18, 1906): 6.

3. F. W. Brown, "Journey to India," *Review and Herald* 76, no. 10 (March 7, 1899): 155.

4. F. W. Brown, "Northwestern India," *Review and Herald* 76, no. 43 (October 24, 1899): 690.

5. A. J. Haysmer, "Death of Brother A. M. Fischer," *Review and Herald* 79, no. 15 (April 15, 1902): 23.

6. Extract from "a private letter" from J. E. Caldwell, quoted in "Raratonga, South Pacific," *Review and Herald* 73, no. 27 (July 7, 1896): 425.

7. A. C. Selmon, "A Call From China," *Review and Herald* 83, no. 26 (June 28, 1906): 12.

8. See D. J. B. Trim, "Ellen G. White and Adventist Mission," in *The Gift of Prophecy in Scripture and History*, ed. Alberto R. Timm and Dwain N. Esmond (Silver Spring, MD: Review and Herald®, 2015), 333–353.

9. Selmon, "A Call From China," 12.

10. E. W. and L. A. Webster, "Trinidad, W. I.," *Review and Herald* 73, no. 27 (July 7, 1896): 424.

11. Selmon, "A Call From China," 12.

12. E. W. Webster, "Trinidad, W. I.,"*Review and Herald* 74, no. 26 (June 29, 1897): 409.

13. Eva Clements's letter printed under title "A Touching Appeal," *Review and Herald* 24, no. 23 (November 15, 1920): 8.